READY-TO-USE EARTH SCIENCE ACTIVITIES for the Elementary Classroom

DEBRA L. SEABURY

THE CENTER FOR APPLIED
RESEARCH IN EDUCATION
West Nyack, New York 10994

Library of Congress Cataloging-in-Publication Data

Seabury, Debra.
Ready-to-use earth science activities for the elementary classroom / Debra L. Seabury
p. cm.
ISBN 0-13-027977-3
1. Environmental sciences—Study and teaching (Elementary)—Activity programs. I. Title.
GE77.S4 1994
372.3'57044—dc20 94-17619
CIP

Printed in the United States of America

10 9 8 7 6 5 4 3 2 1

Originally published as *Earth Smart! Ready-to-Use Environmental Science Activities for the Elementary Classroom* © Copyright 1994 by The Center for Applied Research in Education

ISBN 0-13-027977-3

THE CENTER FOR APPLIED RESEARCH IN EDUCATION
West Nyack, NY 10994

www.phdirect.com

“Never doubt that small groups of thoughtful, committed citizens can change the world. Indeed, it's the only thing that ever has.”

–Margaret Mead

DEDICATION

for Kate and Barbara,
who daily renew my faith in the future.

ABOUT THE AUTHOR

Debra L. Seabury has more than 25 years' experience in elementary and secondary education. She has worked in both classroom and workshop settings with kindergarten to high-school students.

Mrs. Seabury earned her BA from Western Washington University, majoring in elementary education with a minor in English. She has done work in curriculum development and is presently working with middle and high school students while pursuing a graduate degree in literature.

Several of Mrs. Seabury's articles have appeared in *Oasis* magazine. She is co-author with Susan L. Peeples of *Ready-to-Use Science Activities for the Elementary Classroom* (The Center, 1987) and *Ready-to-Use Social Studies Activities for the Elementary Classroom* (The Center, 1989). She is also a member of the editorial advisory board and a contributing author to *The Primary Teacher's Ready-to-Use Activities Program,* published by The Center.

Mrs. Seabury also writes fiction, recently completing her first novel. Her second novel as well as a screenplay are works in progress.

ABOUT THIS RESOURCE

Ready-to-Use Earth Science Activities for the Elementary Classroom gives you fresh, practical, teacher-tested activities to bring the earth sciences alive for your intermediate students. With a wide variety of activity formats designed to enhance many different learning and teaching styles, *Ready-to-Use Earth Science Activities for the Elementary Classroom* explores our unique planet while emphasizing global interdependence and the principles of stewardship. As its interdisciplinary approach reinforces basic reading, writing, and critical thinking skills, this comprehensive resource challenges students to become involved with their own learning, with their own lives and with their own world.

Developed for use with an entire class, small groups, or for individualized instruction, the activities in this resource are readily adaptable to any learning environment—from traditional classrooms to self-paced instructional centers to the specialized situations in accelerated programs. Each activity is complete and ready for immediate use by students for discovery and review.

Ready-to-Use Earth Science Activities for the Elementary Classroom is organized into five sections:

Section One: For the Teacher includes instructions for art and creative writing projects as well as other interactive experiences. Clear, detailed descriptions of all teacher-facilitated activities are supplemented by reproducible forms, calendars, culminating activities, and student awards.

Section Two: Environment—Where are we? is divided into three units exploring land, water, and air. Each unit offers reproducible activities for students, covering such topics as "The Changing Earth," "Rocky Road," "The Water Cycle," and "Up in the Air."

Section Three: Ecology—How do we fit in? is centered around plants, animals, and people. This section focuses on how organisms relate and influence each other within their unique environments. Students will encounter such activities as "Exotic Invaders," "Green Providers," "Plant Survival," and "Classroom Squeeze."

Section Four: Conservation—What can we do? empowers students with an understanding of the allocation of finite resources. Exploring energy use, pollution, and conservation gives students the tools to face a changing world. Topics expanded in this section include "Powerful Decisions," "The Toxic Pyramid," and "Down in the Dumps."

Section Five: Answer Key provides a complete set of answers to all activities found in Sections Two, Three, and Four.

With over 180 pages of reproducible student activities, *Ready-to-Use Earth Science Activities for the Elementary Classroom* offers great flexibility. A comprehensive six-week study of the earth sciences can be planned as simply as a three-week plant unit or a one-week concentration on energy use. Because all activities are laid out step-by-step your preparation is accomplished with maximum efficiency, leaving you more time for quality instruction.

Through interaction with the activities and experiences available in *Ready-to-Use Earth Science Activities for the Elementary Classroom,* you can lead your students through a wide range of concepts and discoveries. Your students will grow in their understanding of earth science, their natural world, and themselves.

Debra L. Seabury

HOW TO USE THIS RESOURCE

Take a few minutes to familiarize yourself with this book and get a feel for its content and structure. *Ready-to-Use Earth Science Activities for the Elementary Classroom* is divided into five sections. Section One is for the teacher and includes a variety of teacher-facilitated activities as well as helpful forms. Sections Two, Three, and Four are made up of reproducible student activities. Section Five offers a complete answer key to all student activity pages.

TEACHER HELPERS

The Resource form, an organizational tool, enables you to keep a list of extra material, information, and contacts. Each time you teach your units, you have only to add new resources. These specific listings eliminate the search for names, numbers, and titles the next time you use your units. In compiling your personal list, be sure to explore online search engines as well as the reference shelves at your public library and your school's media center. Government agencies and professional organizations are good sources of materials and information. Most maintain easily searchable web sites.

The Planning Calendar helps you schedule your units. Reproduce as many pages as necessary to cover the span of your study. After looking over the material in this resource and on your list, select the lesson and activities that best meet your objectives and the needs of your students. Begin filling your calendar. Remember to schedule media and guests well in advance. This is also the time to fit in field trips when and where appropriate.

TEACHER-FACILITATED ACTIVITIES

The teacher-facilitated activities and art projects are integral to each section of this resource. These interactive explorations reinforce the basic content of each unit while leading students to fresh discoveries. These activities and projects show students the real value of their efforts. Most activities include ideas for display and presentation of the end results. Sharing is an important component.

The themes of this book are expanded through creative writing. These writing opportunities move students beyond the basic content and stretch imagination and creativity. Each writing activity is complete with reproducible pages for the presentation of final work. Again, sharing brings students' efforts the attention they deserve.

All too often, units fizzle out with little more than test scores to mark their passings. Culminating activities and student awards keep interest high right up to the last day of your earth science studies. Special events to mark closure leaves your students with positive feelings of accomplishment and helps their learning stay with them.

GETTING STUDENTS STARTED

The student portion has three sections: *Environment, Ecology* and *Conservation.* These sections are further divided into nine units—land, water, air, plants, animals, people, energy, pollution, and conservation. Each unit includes similar varieties of material. Each type of activity is discussed in detail below.

VOCABULARY

Three different types of activities are used in this resource to introduce and expand vocabulary. *Word searches* expose students to new vocabulary specific to the earth sciences. *Crossword puzzles* develop and reinforce the new vocabulary. *Handwriting* pages provide handwriting practice while also reinforcing vocabulary recognition and developing spelling skills. These pages can also be used for recording definitions or writing sentences.

READY-SET-GO ACTIVITIES

The *Ready-Set-Go* selections feature high interest or unusual topics related to specific unit content. Each of these *Ready-Set-Go* activities has a prereading segment, the reading itself, and comprehension checks. Whenever possible, expand the interest these selections generate by displaying related items or additional readings.

MODIFIED CLOZE ACTIVITIES

The modified cloze activities give students information and practice in context word analysis. The student chooses the most appropriate word from a list of choices to complete the article. These short articles lend themselves well to oral reading and are good discussion starters.

RESEARCH ACTIVITIES

The research projects in each of the nine units of *Ready-to-Use Earth Science Activities for the Elementary Classroom* give students opportunities to use a variety of sources in gathering information. Guide students to primary as well as secondary sources, and don't forget online research. Research projects lend themselves well to out-of-class work, small cooperative groups, or enrichment as easily as whole-class involvement.

COOPERATIVE LEARNING

Each of this resource's units includes an activity specifically designed for cooperative learning. These activities encourage students to work together on topics that effect groups of people living together. Some of these activities can be used in cross-age situations expanding your classroom to embrace younger or older student buddies. All cooperative learning activities were developed with the intent to maximize flexibility and expansion options.

MATH ACTIVITIES

Math lessons are content based. Emphasizing basic operations, these activities expand science themes and topics. They are not designed to introduce students to new math concepts, but rather to encourage students to exercise logic and reason in problem-solving.

PUZZLES

A variety of puzzle formats give students opportunities to encounter new information in fresh and engaging ways. Use these puzzles with a whole class, small groups, or individual students. Puzzles also work well in activity centers or as homework assignments to be shared with families.

OTHER REPRODUCIBLE STUDENT ACTIVITIES

Many other activity formats are utilized. These address a wide range of alternate learning styles, and challenge students to grasp information presented visually as well as verbally. Many of these varied activities include suggestions for extended learnings and enrichment work.

QUICK CHECKS

Ready-to-Use Earth Science Activities for the Elementary Classroom uses Quick Checks. Each of the nine units concludes with a one-page review of material specific to that unit. These Quick Checks may be used for pretesting or combined for evaluation of an entire section. They are also useful tools for review practice.

NOTE PAGES

A note page ends each section. These pages lend themselves to a variety of uses. When reproduced, they can be used by the teacher for additional information, and filed with your resources and calendar pages. Students will enjoy taking research notes on copies of these pages as well. You may also choose to write directly in the book to permanently store bits of information on these easily accessible pages.

CONTENTS

About This Resource vi

How to Use This Resource vii

SECTION ONE
FOR THE TEACHER • 1

Resources (reproducible sheet)

Planning Calendar (reproducible sheet)

Activities • 4

Rain in a Glass (4) • Pollution Catchers (4) • The Natural Selection Game (5) • Backward Garden (5) • Energy-Saving Eggs (6) • The Garbage Game (7) • Six Thousand Cans! (7) • Book Swap (8) • A Word About Guests and Field Trips (9)

Art Projects • 10

Endangered Species Trading Cards (10) • New Paper from Old (10) • Sun Paintings (11) • Food Web Mobiles (12) • Brown Bag Posters (12)

Creative Writing • 14

From the Diary of . . . (14) • My Green Commitment (14) • Animal Diamante (15) • Earth Smart News (16)

Awards and Culmination • 21

SECTION TWO: WHERE ARE WE?
ENVIRONMENT • 23

Land

A Land Word Search • 24

Land Handwriting • 25

What's So Special About Earth? • 26

Is Dirt Important? • 27

Where in the World? • 28

The Changing Earth • 30

Rocky Road • 32

More Than Just Dirt • 34
Earth's Resources • 36
Look What I Found! • 38
Your Corner of the World • 40
One Continent? • 41
Coordinate the Coordinates • 42
Land Quick Check • 43

Water

A Water Word Search • 44
Water Handwriting • 45
Where Is All the Water? • 46
Food from the Sea • 47
The Water Cycle • 48
How We Use Water • 50
Turn on the Water • 52
Down the Drain • 54
How Do You Use Water? • 56
Easy Come, Easy Go? • 58
Solar Purifier • 60
Water Use Math • 61
A Watery Puzzle • 62
Water Quick Check • 63

Air

An Air Word Search • 64
Air Handwriting • 65
I Need Some Air • 66
In the Air • 67
Up in the Air • 68
Weather and the Atmosphere • 70

Atmospheric Pressure • 72

Our Changing Climate • 74

Air Pressure Challenge • 76

Great Minds • 78

Hot or Cold? • 80

Air Resistance • 81

An "Airy" Puzzle • 82

Air Quick Check • 83

Environment Notes • 84

SECTION THREE: HOW DO WE FIT IN? ECOLOGY • 85

Plants

A Plant Word Search • 86

Plant Handwriting • 87

The Green Providers • 88

Plant Survival • 89

Portrait of a Plant • 90

Plant Scavenger Hunt • 92

Plant Succession • 94

Special Parts, Special Jobs • 96

Biome Riddles • 98

Tropical Treasure • 100

Scrambled Trees • 102

Transpiration • 103

How Tall? • 104

Plant Quick Check • 105

Animals

An Animal Word Search • 106

Animal Handwriting • 107

Animals, Animals, Animals • 108

Classifying Animals • 109

Battle for Survival • 110

The Balance of Nature • 112

The Clean-Up Crew • 114

Threatened, Endangered, Extinct • 116

Endangered Interview • 118

Animal Products • 120

Exotic Invaders • 122

An Animal Puzzle • 123

Animal Life Spans • 124

Animal Quick Check • 125

People

A Word Search About People • 126

People Handwriting • 127

A Little History • 128

A Little Culture • 129

We Are Unique • 130

World Population Growth • 132

Where Are All the People? • 134

What Are We Doing? • 136

Need or Want? • 138

People and Resources • 140

Surprise Slogan • 142

Classroom Squeeze • 143

Life Expectancy • 144

People Quick Check • 145

Ecology Notes • 146

SECTION FOUR: WHAT CAN WE DO? CONSERVATION • 147

Energy

An Energy Word Search • 148

Energy Handwriting • 149

Energy for the Earth • 150

More and More Energy • 151

Fossil Fuels • 152

Alternative Energy Sources • 154

Making Electricity • 156

Powerful Research • 158

Cars, Cars, Cars • 160

Powerful Decisions • 162

Meter Reader • 164

What R-U? • 165

Powerful Problems • 166

Energy Quick Check • 167

Pollution

A Pollution Word Search • 168

Pollution Handwriting • 169

What Is Pollution? • 170

What a Mess! • 171

What's in the Air? • 172

What's in the Water? • 174

The Toxic Pyramid • 176

Household Hazards • 178

Hazardous Research • 180

Supplies Surprise • 182

Noise, Noise, Noise! • 184

Beach Pickup • 185

Pollution Problems • 186

Pollution Quick Check • 187

<u>Conservation</u>

Wanted: Earth Smart People • 188

Conservation Handwriting • 189

Why Do We Pollute? • 190

Rachel Carson • 191

Down in the Dumps • 192

The Three R's • 194

Why Recycle? • 196

A Draining Experience • 198

An Environmental Issue • 200

The ABC's Go Green • 202

What's Compost? • 204

A Conservation Puzzle • 205

A Little Logic • 206

Conservation Quick Check • 207

Conservation Notes • 208

SECTION FIVE
ANSWER KEY • 209

Section One

FOR THE TEACHER

RESOURCES

★ AUDIO-VISUALS (films, filmstrips, etc.)

number title

_______ ____

_______ ____

_______ ____

_______ ____

★ BOOKS (magazines, prints, transparencies, etc.)

title author/publisher

____________________ ____________________

____________________ ____________________

____________________ ____________________

____________________ ____________________

____________________ ____________________

★ SPEAKERS, FIELD TRIPS, AND OTHER GOODIES

____

____

____

____

____

____

PLANNING CALENDAR

MONDAY	TUESDAY	WEDNESDAY	THURSDAY	FRIDAY

Activities

Rain in a Glass

A sunny day, a glass, and a grassy area can show your students how the water cycle works in our environment. For each student or pair of students you will need a glass and a grassy place where the glass will not be disturbed. The grassy area should be in direct sunlight. Students will also need materials to record their observations.

Have students choose a spot and place their glass upside down on the grass. Students should report observations about the glass and its placement. They might also sketch their experiment. Challenge them to make predictions about what will happen. Leave the glasses undisturbed.

Humidity and temperature will affect the duration of this experiment. Have students check their glasses at regular intervals. They should record their observations. Water molecules from the grass and soil will evaporate. The water vapor will condense on the inside of the glass. A watery film or fog will form first. Eventually "rain" drops will trickle down the inside of the glass. Your students have seen rain in a glass. Help them draw conclusions about the water cycle.

Pollution Catchers

When air looks hazy or smoggy, you are seeing air pollution. Even when you cannot see particles, they are in the air—even indoors! Your students can "catch" this pollution and see how it differs from place to place.

For each student you will need two white index cards, an envelope, and petroleum jelly. Have students smear a thin layer of petroleum jelly on one side of each index card. (The jelly doesn't need to cover the card. A good-sized spot will do.) These cards are now pollution catchers.

Have each student put one catcher inside an envelope and seal it. This will be the control for each experimental location.

Now students are ready to place their pollution catchers. Place the catchers in a variety of locations—inside, outside, near traffic, at home, where food is prepared, etc. Students should write the location on each card or envelope. Be sure to place the sealed envelope and the exposed catcher together. Leave them undisturbed for one week.

Students should check their pollution catchers each day and share their observations with the class. At the end of the week collect and compare the pollution catchers. Open the envelopes and compare with the exposed catchers. Use microscopes or hand lenses, if available. Draw conclusions about locations and the sources of air pollution. You may want to repeat the experiment with different locations to check your conclusions.

The Natural Selection Game

How natural selection favors one characteristic over another is sometimes a difficult concept for students to understand. This game will help students see how a characteristic is influenced by natural selection.

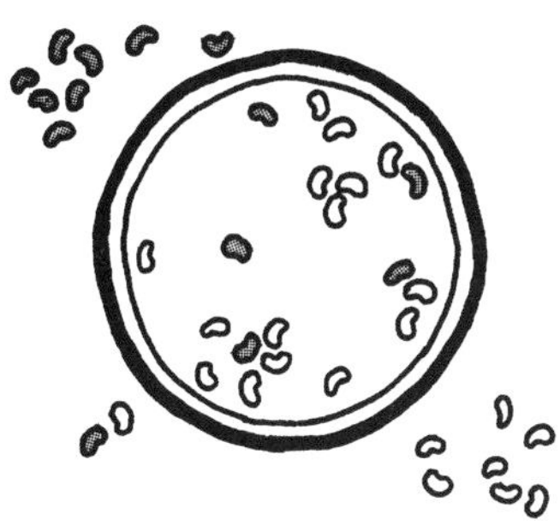

For each pair of students you will need one white paper plate, about 60 small white beans, and about 60 small pinto beans. The paper plate will represent an ecological community. The beans represent an animal specie native to the community. Half of the individuals of the specie are white and half are pinto. The pair of students will play the part of a pair of predators moving into the area.

Begin the natural selection game by explaining the parts of the game and what they represent in a real ecological community. Ask students which of the two colors of beans stands out more from the background of the plate. They should conclude that the pinto beans are easier to see. Have students place 30 beans of each color onto the paper plate representing the community.

Because the pinto beans are easier to see, they are easier for predators to catch. In fact, in this game twice as many pinto prey are caught by the predators than the number of white prey caught. Students hunt by removing beans from the community. Have students hunt and remove beans/prey as they wish, but they must always remove twice as many pinto prey as white prey.

Next, tell students that spring comes and that both the white and pinto prey reproduce. Each pair of prey has three offspring. Add the correct number of beans to the community. Students should continue to hunt, taking twice as many pinto prey as white. Soon students should see that even though they started with 30 of each color, the white prey rapidly out-number the pinto. This is natural selection at work.

If you have an odd number of prey, the odd one fails to find a mate and does not reproduce.

You may want to repeat the game and change some of the variables. Discuss the varied outcomes. Help your students draw conclusions about native animals, camouflage, and natural selection.

Backward Garden

Help your students to recognize materials that are biodegradable by planting a backward garden. You will need a variety of items to plant such as: aluminum foil, a leaf, 100% cotton cloth, an apple core, a piece of paper grocery sack, plastic wrap, a styrofoam cup, a nylon sock, etc. You will also need an area to plant your garden and several ice cream sticks for markers.

Before you have students plant their garden, have them examine the items and make predictions about what might happen to each item. Record the predictions. Make markers for the items by writing the name of each on the end of an ice cream stick with permanent marker.

Students should dig a shallow hole for each item. Place the items in the holes and mark the locations with the labeled ice cream sticks. Cover the holes with soil. Leave your backward garden in the soil for about 5 or 6 weeks. Check it each day and water the garden thoroughly when dry.

After the 5 or 6 weeks have passed, discuss your predictions again. Allow students to add to or change their predictions, as they wish. Now dig up your backward garden and examine each item. Use hand lenses if available. Have students note their observations. What has happened to each item? What items changed the most? What do these items have in common? Which items changed the least? Help students draw conclusions about the biodegradibility of natural and man-made items.

Energy-Saving Eggs

Saving energy isn't always difficult or painful. You simply need to be energy smart. Much of the energy we use is actually wasted. Boiling some eggs can show your students how to be energy smart and do the job with the least energy possible.

For this demonstration you will need an even number of eggs. Two eggs will do. However, since cooking without eating isn't much fun, try to use at least half as many eggs as you have students. You will also need two pans of the same size, a lid to fit one of the pans, a stopwatch or clock with a second hand and several butter knives. For heat, you will need two burners of the same size. Either a stove or hot plate will work. You may also want some crackers to serve with the cooked eggs.

To begin, have students measure equal amounts of water into each pot. (There should be enough water to cover the eggs when they are added to the pots later.) Put each pot on a burner. Put the lid on one pot. Turn the burners on high. Time how long it takes for the water in each pot to boil. You will need to listen for the pot with the lid, because removing the lid to peek will allow heat to escape. Record how long it takes for each pot to come to a boil.

When both pots are boiling carefully place an equal number of eggs into each pot. Replace the lid and turn the heat under the covered pot down to a gentle simmer. Leave the burner under the uncovered pot on high. Boil the eggs for 10 minutes. Turn off the burners and drain the water from the eggs. To cool the eggs quickly, refill the pans with cold water and wait 10 minutes. While you wait, disuss the demonstration. Ask students to predict which eggs are cooked the most and tell why they think so. Which pan used more energy? How do you know?

When the eggs are cool enough to handle, give each pair of students an egg. Be sure that they know which pan their egg came from. Students should peel the eggs and cut them in half length-wise. Compare the eggs and students' predictions. Help students to see that all the eggs are cooked the same. Explain that once water boils, it remains 100 degrees C. No matter how furiously it boils, it remains 100 degrees C. The only difference in the eggs is how much energy is wasted. Enjoy the eggs.

The Garbage Game

Garbage doesn't go away. Often it is a case of out of sight, out of mind. The garbage game will show your students that no matter where we throw it, the amount of garbage stays the same. Students will also get some exercise and brush up their addition skills.

Before you play the garbage game, you will need some clean garbage. Have your students collect milk cartons. Asking for the cooperation of other classes or your lunchroom staff will get you more "garbage" in a shorter time. Students should wash out the cartons thoroughly and allow them to dry. The game works best if you have several times as many cartons as you have students.

To play the game use your desks or tables to divide your classroom into four areas to represent four communities. Assign about the same number of student/citizens to each community. Dump about the same amount of cartons/garbage in each community. Tell students that you want them to dispose of their garbage by dumping it across the desks into another community. Tell them that they can get rid of trash until you give the signal to stop. Demonstrate the signal. Flashing the lights is a good signal as the game can get a bit noisy.

When the garbage dumping stops, have students count their cartons. Generally, children will immediately declare winners. Simply ignore them and enlist their help in totaling all the teams' counts on the board. Repeat the game again and total all the cartons. Repeat until the students realize that the total will always remain the same. They have NOT gotten rid of the garbage—only moved it around. Help them draw conclusions about the garbage we make on the earth. Have them suggest better ways of handling waste disposal.

Six Thousand Cans!

The average American family of four disposes of the equivalent of 6,000 aluminum soft drink cans each year! All of these cans could be recycled. We would not only preserve our limited supply of aluminum, but save huge amounts of power as well. Recycling an aluminum can uses only 5% of the energy needed to make a new can.

Show your students what 6,000 cans look like and start them on the road to recycling. Begin by discussing the use of aluminum cans and their disposal. Tell students that each year the average American family tosses away 6,000 cans. Have students predict what that many cans might look like. How much space would 6,000 aluminum cans take up in a landfill? How long do they think it would take your class to collect 6,000 aluminum cans?

Let students devise plans for gathering cans. Will they bring them from home? Should they put collection boxes in other classrooms? Lunchroom? Local business? Also have students plan how to count cans and keep track of their progress. You may want to have daily or weekly can updates. Graphing works well here, too.

While students are collecting cans, study recycling and how recycled cans are turned into new products. Invite a representative from your local waste disposal company to visit your class and talk about your community's systems for waste collection and recycling.

When you have reached your goal, stack the cans and measure the pile. Compare to the predictions you made earlier. Recycling these cans will save aluminum, energy, and the space in a landfill. Encourage your students to continue saving cans to recycle (and maybe other recyclables, too).

Most recycling centers pay for scrap aluminum. Recycle your cans at one that does and let students decide how to use the income to improve the environment. Maybe they can plant something green on your school grounds, buy a book about environmental issues for your school library, contribute to an organization that helps endangered animals, or...?

Book Swap

Things we are no longer interested in usually end up in landfills and incinerators. Often these items are still useful. Your students can have a book swap and see how easily things they no longer want can be put to use by someone else.

Your book swap can be as simple or as elaborate as you choose. The basics are quite simple. Students bring books that they no longer want and trade for others that interest them.

Discuss the idea of a book swap with your class. Make decisions about how your swap should work. You may want to limit the number of books each person may bring. Three to five books per person is quite manageable. Perhaps you will want to swap only paperbacks or just fiction. Discuss with students how and when the swap will take place. Set a day and time.

You will want to send a note to parents including pertinent information and a permission slip to return with space to list the books their child will be bringing to swap.

On the day of the book swap, you may want to have a few paperbacks of your own available to trade. This way you can include students who may not have brought any books to trade. Students can put their books out on their desks. Allow time to browse and discuss choices. Some children may want to do brief booktalks on a few selected titles. Let children trade while you circulate to facilitate transactions.

After the book swap is complete, allow time for children to read their new books. Later discuss what students thought about the swap. What was best? What could be changed to make it better? You may want to wait a month or two and have another book swap. If you have room in your classroom, you can set up an on-going book exchange. Start with a dozen or so books. Allow students to bring a book and trade for one from the shelf whenever they like. This way they can continue to change old books into new ones.

A Word About Guests and Field Trips

Some of your best resources are in your own community. Many individuals as well as organizations are more than willing to share their expertise. Businesses, government agencies, professional groups, colleges, parks, museums, and clubs are good resources. Many will share materials, conduct special tours, or send speakers to your class. Your students' families may have related hobbies or interests they would enjoy sharing. Enthusiasm is contagious!

Whether for a speaker or field trip, prepare your students to be courteous and receptive. A list of pertinent questions may be helpful. Remember that guests and outings provide valuable experiences for your students. At the same time, they give people who are not ordinarily connected to your school a chance to see education at work. Last, always remember to have students thank community members. A poster, letter, or artwork signed by each class member would be just right.

Art Projects

Endangered Species Trading Cards

Capitalize on your students' interest in trading cards to introduce them to some endangered species. Each student should work with a different endangered animal. They will need to research some basic facts and locate at least one clear picture of their animal.

Students should create original blackline drawings of their endangered animals. Pictures should not be larger than 4" by 5 1/2". Use white paper and your choice of markers, pen and ink, or even soft-lead drawing pencils. Because these drawings will be reproduced, encourage children to make them as clear as possible and erase cleanly. These drawings will be the fronts of the trading cards.

For the back of each trading card, students should hand letter pertinent information. You will want the name of the animal and its native habitat. You may want other facts about its size and color as well as its particular ecological problem. Printing for the back of the card should fill a space no larger then 4" x 5 1/2".

When students have finished their original backs and fronts, you will be ready to make masters for reproduction. Paste students' art on 8 1/2" x 11" paper. Rubber cement works well. You will be able to put four drawings on each master. Be sure fronts and backs match. Run copies on card stock. Cut apart to make individual cards. Make several sets. You may wish to have the artists color and sign their cards.

Divide your class into several groups. Give each group a set of cards. Have students make up games using the endangered trading cards. Allow each group to teach their best game to the class. Arrange for your class to teach games to a class of younger children. Make a gift of a set of cards to the other class. Keep at least one set of cards in your classroom for free-time use.

New Paper from Old

One of the best ways for your students to learn about recycling paper is to recycle some themselves. Junk mail can be turned into sheets of writing paper in your classroom.

Have your students save junk mail at home and bring it to school. They will need to sort the paper to take out any plastic windows or really shiny paper. These will not recycle well. Have students tear the paper for recycling into pieces about 1-inch square. In addition to the torn paper you will need a bucket, a large bowl, a blender, a large pan at least three inches deep, a piece of fine wire mesh to fit the pan, water, and absorbent cloths.

Begin by soaking the torn pieces of junk mail in a bucket of water overnight. The next day, pour off any excess water. Add about an equal amount of water, put the lid on the blender, and blend to liquify. Pour the pulp into a large bowl. Continue to blend the pulp in small batches and add to the bowl.

Pour about an inch of water into the large pan. Add about two cups of pulp. Stir to mix. Slide the piece of wire mesh into the pan and lift. The mesh should be covered with a thin coat of pulp. This part can be a bit tricky. You may need to add pulp or water until you get the desired effect.

When you have a thin coat of pulp on the wire mesh, carefully turn it pulp-side down on an absorbent cloth. Press down hard and then peel off the mesh, leaving the pulp on the cloth. Place another cloth on top of the pulp sheet. Repeat with the remaining pulp.

After you have finished stacking the pulp sheets and cloths, pile some heavy books on top. Use a plastic bag to protect the books. Leave the pile undisturbed overnight. The next day, gently peel the sheets of paper from the cloths. Put the new paper sheets on newspaper to continue drying. When your paper is dry, it's ready to use. Use it to make note cards, thank-you's, or invitations. Mark the back "Recycled Paper Made by ____________________."

SUN PAINTINGS

Show your students the power of the sun by making silhouette pictures with sun power. You will need vivid-colored paper. Black, purple, and royal blue work well. You will also need a number of small items with interesting shapes. Gloves and pipe cleaners seem to be particularly fun. You may also use cut-outs in place of or in addition to the small items.

This project must be done on a sunny day. The more direct the sunlight, the more dramatic your results will be. You may choose to work outdoors, but the effect works equally well on a sunny windowsill. Just be sure that sunlight will strike your pictures directly for several hours.

Begin by asking students if they have ever seen something that has been faded by the sun. Discuss the power of the sun's energy and explain that the sun can "paint" a picture with your help. Place pieces of vivid construction paper in direct sunlight. Encourage students to place items on the paper in an interesting arrangement. Leave the pictures undisturbed. The amount of fading depends on the duration and angle of the sunlight. You may like to start this project on a Friday and leave it over a sunny weekend. If you put out a test picture with many small squares of paper, you can periodically remove a square to check how the fading is progressing. Use this to judge when the sun paintings are ready.

Have the students remove the items they placed on their picture. They should have clear silhouettes of the items. Mat the sun paintings with coordinating-colored mats and display around a large cut-out of the sun with the title "Sun Paintings."

FOOD WEB MOBILES

Reinforce your students' study of food webs and interdependence by creating eye-catching mobiles. Let them learn a bit about balance, too. Decide if you would like students to work in groups, pairs, or individually on this project. For each mobile you will need at least three branches, index cards, and yarn.

Begin by discussing food webs. Be sure students understand the terms: producer, primary consumer, and secondary consumer. (See student activity, "The Balance of Nature.") On index cards, have students draw pictures for each level of the food chain. You may choose to have them cut pictures from magazines and glue the pictures to the index cards. Be sure to have a picture for each side of the cards. Use a paper punch to make a hole at the top of each card. Tie a piece of yarn through the hole on each card.

To assemble the mobile, begin with the producers. These should be tied to one of the branches. Experiment and find a balance point of the branch. Attach a piece of yarn at the balance. Tie the primary consumers to another branch. Find the balance point of the branch and attach another piece of yarn. Repeat for the secondary consumers. Assemble the three parts of the mobile by attaching each level to the one above with yarn. Adjust to balance the finished mobile. Display by hanging in your classroom or school media center. Make a sign with the title "Food Web Mobiles by ________________" to complete the display.

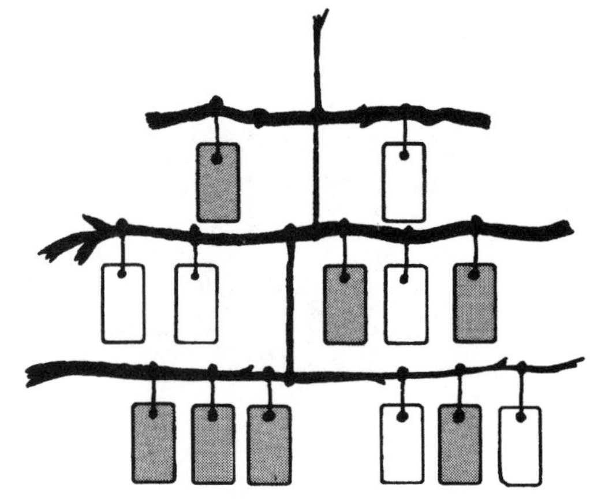

BROWN BAG POSTERS

Focus students' attention on what they, as individuals, can do to help preserve our environment by making posters of recycled materials. Use the posters to spread the word about being earth smart.

Discuss posters as an art form. Show some posters. Note layout, use of slogans, and visual impact. Help students see how some posters are more effective in conveying their messages than others. Explain that students will be making posters to help show other children and adults how to be earth smart. Brainstorm ideas for poster themes. Help each student to choose a topic. You will need a brown grocery bag for each student. You will also need scraps of colored paper, fabric or other used materials, glue, and scissors.

Students should begin by drafting their poster designs. For this purpose use the back sides of classroom waste paper. Because finished posters will be made of cut paper and fabric, encourage simple designs. Remind children that they are saving trees by using wasted paper and used bags.

For the finished posters, use brown grocery bags. Cut the bags along seams and open flat. Use the inside for the poster. Cut shapes from paper and/or fabric to complete designs. Glue the designs to the brown bag. Encourage students to experiment before gluing their finished work. Some students may choose to cut letters for their slogans, but lettering with crayons or markers is also acceptable and much simpler. You may want to take the opportunity to discuss art supplies that are earth friendly. Display the finished posters around your school where other students and staff will see them and learn to be earth smart.

Creative Writing

Creative writing is an important component in any interdisciplinary unit. Writing challenges students to synthesize information and integrate new ideas with what they already know and believe.

Help students to be successful in their writing by brainstorming ideas, words, facts, and observations. List these on the board or overhead. Accept everything students offer and add your own impressions as well. In writing rough drafts the important thing is to get the ideas on paper. Have students reread their writing to themselves and share them. Encourage them to refine their work. After self-editing, students should proof their work with an adult. Check for grammar, spelling, and punctuation.

Use the reproducible student pages for final copies. Students put a great deal into their writing, so it is important that the presentation of the finished products be worthy of their efforts. Attempt to find display ideas that will let students share their writing with classmates, families, the school, and the larger community.

FROM THE DIARY OF . . .

Students can move away from their own point of view by writing a diary for a plant or creature in their environment. Help students choose subjects for their diaries. Discuss diaries as a writing form. Share some famous diaries. Suggest that these writings often include feelings, opinions, and personal thoughts. Help students develop the point of view of their subjects through brainstorming. Encourage them to include comments about habitat, community, and ecology from their subjects' point of view.

Allow time for students to write entries in their diaries each day for at least a week. They may write on notebook paper or in a journal, if you use them. When diaries are complete, have students reread their entries and choose one entry that they would like to share. You may allow them to combine thoughts from two or more entries. Proofread, edit, and polish these entries.

Provide students with copies of "From the Diary of ..." Have students write their final copies of their chosen entries. Children can share their diary entries orally. Make copies of all the children's final copy entries and bind them in a book for your classroom. Original copies should be returned to the student authors.

MY GREEN COMMITMENT

Students can reflect on what they have learned about the environment and human behavior by writing their own personal commitments to being earth smart. Discuss pledges and oaths. Share examples such as the 4-H Pledge, the Scout Pledge, or an oath of office. You may want to share the Declaration of Independence as well. Help students see how these writings promise certain behaviors and commitments.

Brainstorm with your class things that each of us can do to help preserve the natural environment. Encourage them to reflect on what they really want to commit themselves to. Which things do they believe are most important? What will they continue to do?

Allow time to write rough drafts of students' commitments. Proofread and edit the rough drafts. Supply student sheets, "My Green Commitment," for each student's finished copy. You may want to reproduce the student sheets on pastel green or even parchment paper. Students should sign their commitments and share them with classmates. If possible, invite your principal or other dignitaries to listen in. You or your principal should sign as a witness. An official-looking stamp or seal would be a great addition. Display these commitments in a hallway or window where visitors to your school can read and enjoy them.

Animal Diamante

Use a simplified diamante or diamond-shaped poem to have students develop skills with description. This simplified form has seven lines. The form and a sample poem are shown below. You may want to collaborate on a few group poems to help students become comfortable with the form.

Brainstorming helps generate a wide variety of subject possibilities. Have each student write several poems. Students may work individually or in pairs. The students' best efforts should go on the "Animal Diamante" final form. Mount these poems on diamonds of blue and green construction paper. Punch a hole in the top corner and use a piece of brown yarn to hang for display. You may want to mount these back to back or have students make illustrations for the back sides.

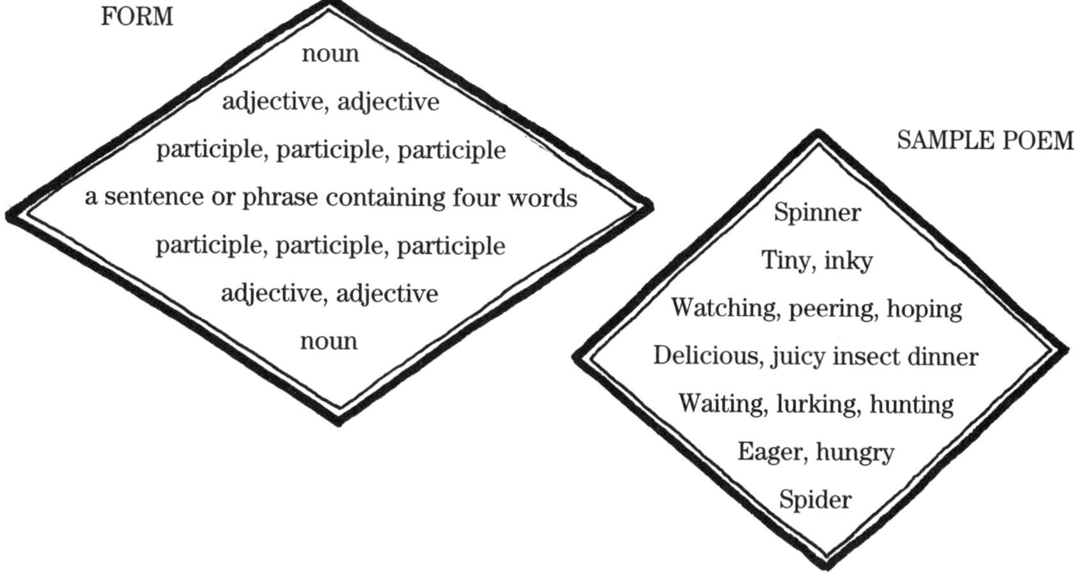

EARTH SMART NEWS

Your students can spread the word about the environment by becoming reporters for the *Earth Smart News*. Begin by having students read and discuss several short news articles. Help them notice the headlines and writing styles. Explain that they will be writing news articles for the *Earth Smart News*.

Have students choose and research environmental issues. These issues may be local, regional, national, or global. Encourage children to include details about how the issues will affect them and their families. Also address what is being done about the issues. Help them polish their articles.

Students should copy their edited articles onto the *Earth Smart News* pages. Students should add an illustration, graph, or other visual in the space provided. Each article also needs a catchy headline. Reproduce finished articles back to back and staple to make completed copies of your newspaper.

Original articles should be returned to students. Distribute copies of your newspaper to other classes who share your interest in the earth.

THE DIARY OF . . .

MY "GREEN" COMMITMENT

signed by: ______________________________

witnessed by: ______________________________

date: ______________________________

ANIMAL DIAMANTE

Cut along this line for display.

, , , ,

by:

★ EARTH ★ SMART ★ NEWS ★

☆ SPECIAL EDITION FOR ENVIRONMENTAL ISSUES ☆

HEADLINE:

BYLINE

Awards and Culmination

These awards may be used at the end of your environmental unit and all along the way. The band awards below may be used as bracelets or bookmarks. For bracelets simply tape one end of the band to the other to fit the student's wrist. The small awards on the next page can be used as tokens redeemable for prizes or privileges as well as simply for positive recognition. A personal note on the back of these awards makes them even more special. The half-page certificate on the next page is designed to recognize students' achievements in completing their environmental studies.

Upon the completion of the study of the environment, you will have a collection of booklets, writing, activities, and art projects. To make the culmination of your work really special, plan an earth fair or picnic. Emphasize earth-smart planning. Use durable plates and supplies. Buy food items in bulk to eliminate packaging.

At your fair, display children's art and projects. Share stories and reports. Have children demonstrate experiments and activities. Play cooperative group games. Invite families or other classes. If your school grounds are limited, a nearby park would be a good location. Celebrate and congratulate your students in taking a big step toward becoming earth smart!

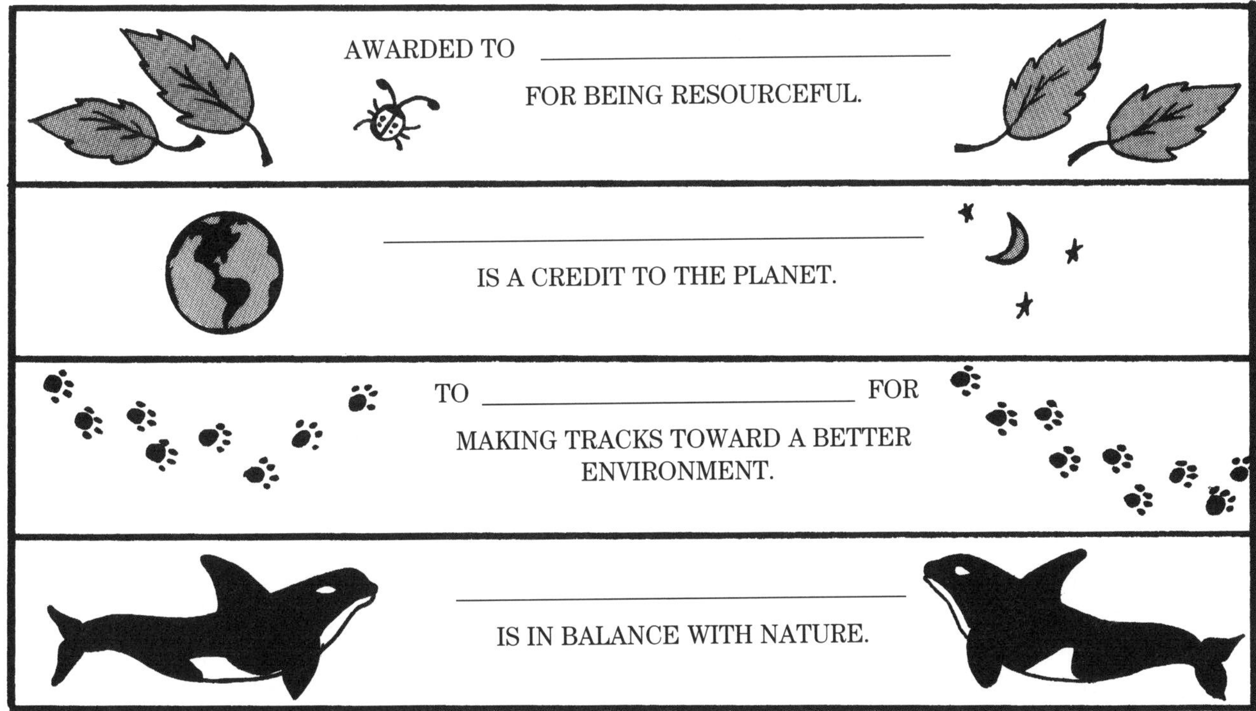

Let it be known on this ________ day of ________________ in the year ____________ that this individual has shown great effort and wisdom in the study of our environment and the interdependence of all living things. Go forth and share what you have learned for the good of your family, your community, and your world.

signed by ____

witnessed by ____

Section Two

Where Are We?

ENVIRONMENT

Name ______________________________

A LAND WORD SEARCH

Circle each of the words you find in the word search. The words can be found either down or across.

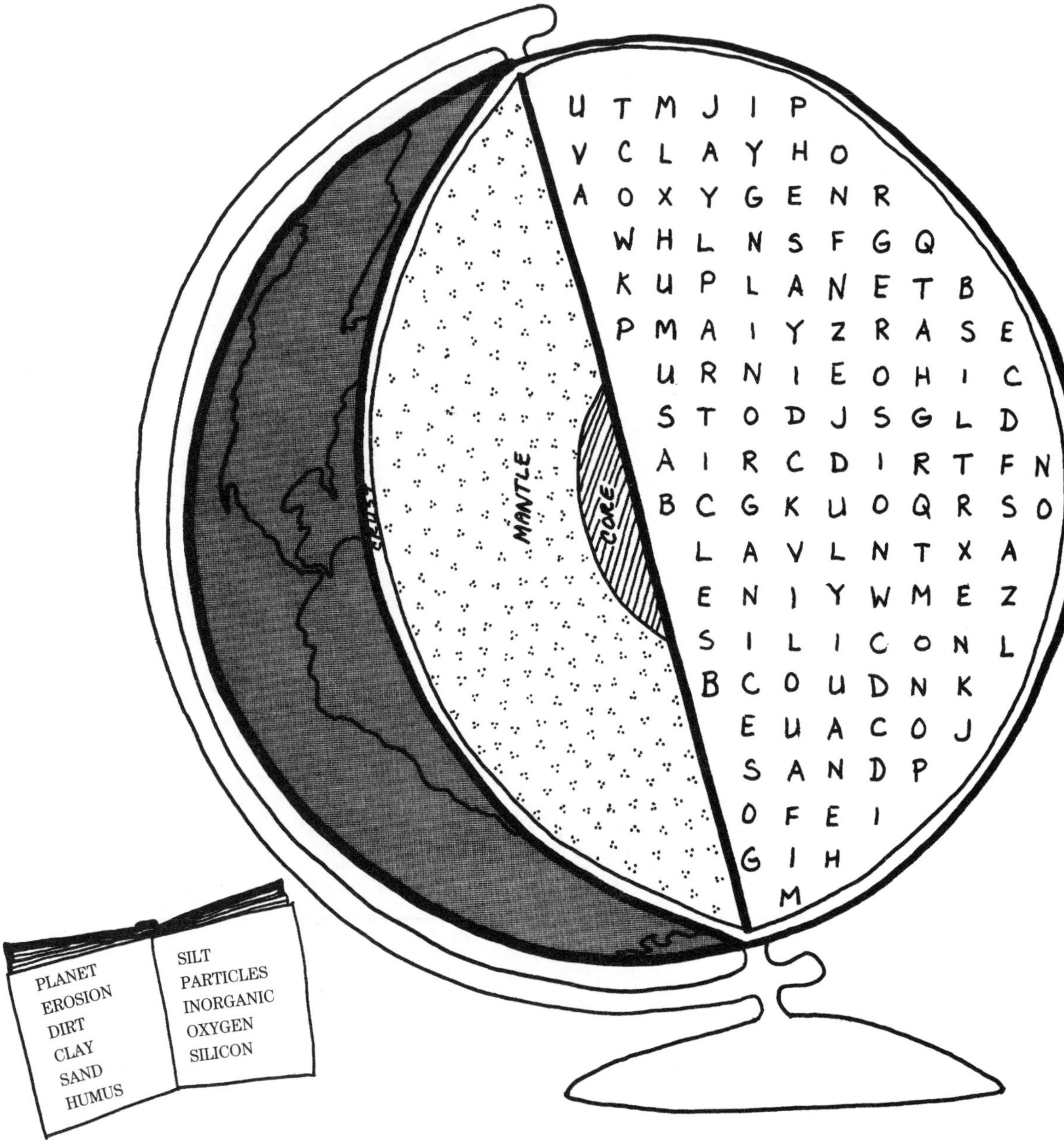

U T M J I P
V C L A Y H O
A O X Y G E N R
W H L N S F G Q
K U P L A N E T B
P M A I Y Z R A S E
U R N I E O H I C
S T O D J S G L D
A I R C D I R T F N
B C G K U O Q R S O
L A V L N T X A
E N I Y W M E Z
S I L I C O N L
B C O U D N K
E U A C O J
S A N D P
O F E I
G I H
M

PLANET
EROSION
DIRT
CLAY
SAND
HUMUS
SILT
PARTICLES
INORGANIC
OXYGEN
SILICON

Name____________________________________

LAND HANDWRITING

environment ____________________________________

____

volcanic ____________________________________

____

earthquake ____________________________________

____

magma ____________________________________

____

formation ____________________________________

____

tectonics ____________________________________

____

minerals ____________________________________

____

igneous ____________________________________

____

sedimentary ____________________________________

____

metamorphic ____________________________________

____

Name ______________________________

WHAT'S SO SPECIAL ABOUT EARTH?

As you read this story, circle the correct word in each numbered box at the bottom of this sheet.

As planets go, our earth is small. It is only about 25,000 miles around. Our solar 1.____________ is not the largest and our sun is only a medium size 2.____________. What is so special about the Earth? It is the only 3.____________ we know about that has just the right environment for plants, 4.____________, and people to live and grow. Of all the stars, planets, and moons studied by scientists, only Earth is just right!

Earth has the perfect balance of elements to 5.___________ life. The Earth's atmosphere moderates the temperatures in our environment. Plants, animals, and people can live only in a narrow range of 6.____________. Venus, one of our nearest neighbors in space, is far too hot. We 7._________ freeze on Mars. Even our closet neighbor, the Moon, has temperatures far too severe for us to survive.

Our earth is the only planet with liquid water. 9.________ is necessary for all life processes. You are about 70% water! No where else is the water we need available. It is all right here.

We also need just the right air. Plants need the 10.________ elements in the air to make their food from the sunshine. People and animals need oxygen and give off carbon dioxide. Plants need carbon dioxide and give off oxygen. Life on Earth is in a delicate balance. All the elements necessary for life are present only on our earth. The Earth is very special. It is our home.

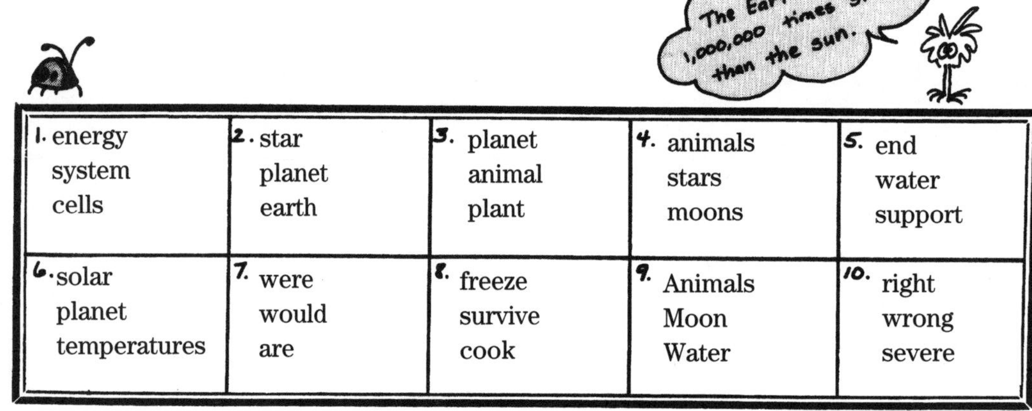

1. energy system cells	2. star planet earth	3. planet animal plant	4. animals stars moons	5. end water support
6. solar planet temperatures	7. were would are	8. freeze survive cook	9. Animals Moon Water	10. right wrong severe

Name_______________________________

IS DIRT IMPORTANT?

As you read this story, circle the correct word in each numbered box at the bottom of this sheet.

Next to air, dirt or soil is the most common thing in our environment. Every 1.__________ thing depends on dirt for food. You don't eat dirt, of course, but you can eat plants. The meat you 2.____________ is fed plants and plants couldn't grow without soil.

Soil is the thin 3.________ of sand, clay, and humus that covers most of the earth's crust. Soil begins to form when 4._________ and minerals are broken down by forces in the environment. Wind, rain, glaciers, and rivers all 5. ________ up the bedrock. Freezing and thawing are also powerful forces that crumble 6._________. It takes a very, very 7._____________ time for rich soil to develop.

Plant and animal matter decay and form humus in the 8.________. Bacteria in the soil helps dead plant and 9._________ matter to break down. This releases nutrients into the 10.________. Over hundreds of years the humus mixes with the crumbled rock, silt, sand, and clay to form rich, fertile soil.

The next time you are in a park or forest, look on the ground for dead leaves. Gently brush some aside and look for last year's leaves or the leaves from the year before. You are watching soil form!

1. dead living rocky	2. eat plant dirt	3. layer rock environment	4. meat wind rocks	5. eat grow break
6. plants animals rocks	7. short living long	8. soil river wind	9. animal mineral Earth	10. soil water air

WHERE IN THE WORLD?

Follow the directions below to complete your "Where in the World?" map.

1. Label the seven continents. They are EUROPE, ASIA, NORTH AMERICA, SOUTH AMERICA, AFRICA, AUSTRALIA, and ANTARCTICA.

2. Label the four oceans. They are ATLANTIC OCEAN, PACIFIC OCEAN, ARCTIC OCEAN, and INDIAN OCEAN.

3. Mark the compass rose with the ordinal directions. Use N, E, S, and W to show north, east, south, and west.

4. Label two bodies of water that are not oceans.

5. Label two islands.

6. Make up a symbol for mountains. Use your symbol to show the locations of three large mountains. Label them with their names.

7. Put a red star where you live. Label the nearest city or town.

8. Use blue stars to show three places you would like to visit. Label these places. If you have already visited one of these places, circle its star.

9. Lightly color blue the water areas of your map. Colored pencils would work well.

10. Lightly color green the land areas of your map.

11. Locate three features on your map that are not already labeled. Find out their names and label them.

Name________________________________

WHERE IN THE WORLD?, CONTINUED

Name ______________________________

THE CHANGING EARTH

Ready:

volcanic
Earthquakes
molten
magma
redepositing
dissolves
Evaporation
spectacular
formations
erosion

1. "Melted" means almost the same as ____________________.
2. Sugar or salt ________________________ in water so you can't see it anymore.
3. The root word of ______________________ is "deposit."
4. ___________________ is the process of water changing to water vapor.
5. ______________________________is a compound word.
6. Molten rock under the surface of the earth is called ____________________________.

Set:

When you look around, you will see many things moving. People, animals, insects, and birds move. The air moves. Trees sway in the breeze. The grass ripples and water flows. However, we rarely think of the earth itself moving.

The earth is moving and changing all the time. Some changes such as volcanic eruptions and earthquakes happen quickly. Most changes are much slower—so slow that we hardly notice them. The earth is constantly changing. Land is being worn away and new land is being built up. These changes may take hundreds, thousands or even <u>hundreds</u> of thousands of years!

Land is built up by pressure from deep inside the earth. The crust of earth is actually made up of huge plates that float on top of molten rock. These plates collide, bulge, and wrinkle. Mountains are pushed up and land masses grow. Volcanoes form where cracks in the earth's crust allow magma to reach the surface. When parts of the earth's crust move suddenly, we call it an earthquake.

While the earth is constantly being built up, it is also being worn away. Many forces in the environment erode or wear away the surface of the earth. Water is a major force of erosion. Rain beats on the earth, loosens soil, and carries it down slopes. Rivers eat at their banks and waves nibble shorelines. Water also dissolves minerals found in some rock. The minerals are carried by the water until evaporation causes the water to leave the minerals behind. Limestone caves, stilactites, and stilagmites are caused by this process.

Temperature also plays a part in erosion. Water seeps into cracks in rock. The freezing water makes it expand or get bigger. This breaks up the rock and loosens pieces that later are carried away. Glaciers of compressed snow and ice move huge boulders and vast amounts of soil.

Name________________________________

THE CHANGING EARTH, CONTINUED

Wind is a powerful force of erosion. Winds pick up soil and carry it many miles before redepositing it in new places. While the wind is moving soil is also scouring the exposed earth like a sand blaster. Spectacular formations in the Grand Canyon are the result of blowing sand.

Take a close look around. Can you see the earth move?

1. Most changes in the earth happen very, very (quickly, slowly).

2. Two types of changes in the earth can happen quickly. They are ______________________ and ______________________.

3. The earth's crust is actually made up of huge plates floating on molten rock. (TRUE, FALSE)

4. ______________________, ______________________ and ______________________ are all forces that cause erosion.

5. ______________________ found in some rocks are dissolved by water and carried away.

6. Wind moves ______________________ and redeposits it in new places.

7. How does temperature cause erosion?____

____

____

____

____

____

Name ______________________________

ROCKY ROAD

1. "Sediment" is the root word found in the word ______________________________.

mineral inorganic ingneous pumice continuously sedimentary metamorphic oxygen silicon quartz

2. ________________________ begins with the same sound as the word "otter."

3. __________________ and ______________ both begin with the "i" sound in the word "it."

4. If something goes on all the time, it happens ______________________________.

5. In the word ____________________ , "ph" makes the "f" sound.

The earth is continuously changing, building, and wearing away. The earth's building blocks are minerals. Minerals are the inorganic (non-living) solids found in the natural world. Minerals combine to form the rock that makes up the earth's crust. We stand around on chunks of minerals!

There are many minerals but just eight different minerals make up more than 98% of all rock. The important eight are oxygen, silicon, aluminum, iron, calcium, sodium, potassium, and magnesium. A few rocks like quartz are made up of only one mineral, but most rock is a mixture of minerals.

Rocks are formed in three different ways. When molten magma from deep in the earth cools and hardens, igneous rock is formed, much like fudge cooling in your own kitchen. Hard, glassy obsidian rock forms when magma cools very quickly. Pumice is cooled lava with many air bubbles. Igneous rock is common in areas with a history of volcanic activity.

Another way rock builds up is in layers like the layers in a sandwich. Layering produces sedimentary rock. Fast-moving rivers can carry along dirt, sand, pebbles, and other materials.

The fast-moving water carries alot. As the water slows down, it cannot hold as much material. The dirt, sand, and other things are dropped to the bottom. You can see how this happens by stirring a teaspoon of dirt into a glass of water. When you stop stirring, the particles of dirt settle to the bottom of the glass. Over a long period of time layers build up, one on top of another. These layers are compressed by more layers. The layers harden into sedimentary rock. Shale and limestone are sedimentary rock.

Name ______________________________

ROCKY ROAD, CONTINUED

Fossils are found in sedimentary rock where plants or animals become trapped in the rock layers. Much of the rock in the mid-sections of North America is sedimentary rock.

The third kind of rock is called metamorphic rock. "Meta" means change and "morphic" means form. Metamorphic rock is rock that has changed form, usually because of heat or pressure. Heat from deep in the earth bakes sedimentary or igneous rock and makes metamorphic rock. This works a bit like your oven baking dough into bread. Marble and slate are metamorphic rock. Look carefully at the rocks near where you live. Try to find out if they are igneous, sedimentary, or metamorphic.

Go:

1. Minerals are (organic, inorganic) solids found in the natural world.

2. Just eight different minerals make up more than ______________________ of all rock.

3. Rocks are formed in (many, eight, three) different ways.

4. Cooled magma forms ______________________ rock, such as obsidian.

5. Layers of sediment build up to form ______________________ rock such as limestone.

6. Rock changed by heat or pressure is called ______________________ rock.

7. Silicon and aluminum are metamorphic rock. (TRUE, FALSE)

8. Most rocks are made up of a mixture of ______________________.

Name ______________________________

MORE THAN JUST DIRT

Soil differs greatly from one location to another. A handful of beach sand feels very different from a handful of garden soil. All soil is made of tiny bits of the rocks and minerals that crumbled to form the soil in the beginning.

There are three types of particles of soil. Sand is made up of the largest particles of soil. Sand feels gritty between your fingers. Silt is made up of the next smaller particles of soil. You can see the largest silt particles if you look very closely, but you would need a microscope to see the smallest bits. Clay is made up of the finest particles of soil. Wet clay feels slippery or sticky between your fingers. Dry clay is hard, crusty, or brittle.

The three types of soil also have different weights. You can do an experiment to show which type of soil is heaviest. Put soil that is a mixture of sand, silt, and clay into a jar filled with water. Shake the jar to mix the soil and water. Then set the jar where it won't be disturbed. After several hours, you will see layers have formed. At the bottom will be sand, which is the heaviest type of soil. A layer of clay will be in the middle. Silt, with the lightest weight, will be on top. It may be hard to see the layers of clay and silt, but if you carefully remove samples you should be able to feel the difference.

Most dirt is a mixture of all three types of soil. Different mixtures are best for different uses. Clay is used for making bricks and pottery because it sticks together and dries hard. Sand is heated with small amounts of lime and soda to make glass. Certain crops grow better in one soil mix than another. It is important for people to know what type of soil is found in a certain area. Many farmers can tell you the type of soil mix just by feeling it!

Clay alone is not good for growing plants. It is too hard for roots to push through. Water doesn't drain well from clay soil. Sand has too much space between particles for it to hold enough water. It is difficult for roots to take hold in sand. Silt alone is so light that wind easily blows it away. A mixture of all three kinds of soil is best for growing plants. The richest kind of dirt is called loam. Loam is dirt with lots of silt, some clay, and a small amount of sand. Many food crops grow well in loam.

Name____________________________

MORE THAN JUST DIRT, CONTINUED

Use one of these three words to fill each of the blank spaces on this page.

1. What type of soil has the largest particles? ______________________________

2. What type of soil has medium-sized particles? ______________________________

3. What type of soil has the smallest particles? ______________________________

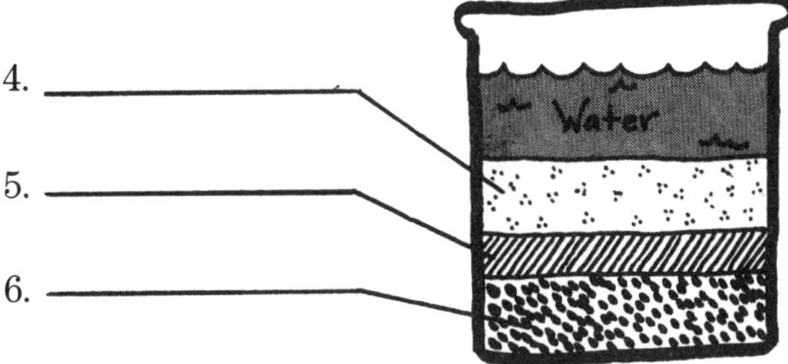

7. ____________ all by itself is too hard for plants' roots to push through.

8. ____________ feels gritty when rubbed between your fingers.

9. ____________ is heavier than silt, but not as heavy as sand.

10. ____________ is the type of soil with medium-sized particles and the lightest weight.

11. ____________ by itself is so light that the wind can easily blow it away.

12. ____________ has too much space between particles to hold very much for very long.

13. ____________ is heated with small amounts of lime and soda to make glass.

14. ____________ is used to make bricks and pottery because it sticks together and dries hard.

 On the back of this sheet describe what loam is and why it is important. 

Name ______________________________

EARTH'S RESOURCES

Our earth is able to support life because certain special things are found here. Land, water, and air are important natural resources. Natural resources are all the things found on the earth that people need and use.

One kind of natural resource is biological or living. Biological resources include all plants and animals. These are the most basic and important resources. All the earth's food comes from plants and animals. Plants give off oxygen and trees provide shelter.

Mineral resources are things like metals, sand, stone, and fossil fuels. These resources are important energy and raw materials. Fossil fuels power factories, homes, and cars. Mineral resources provide the raw materials for televisions, bicycles, and airplanes.

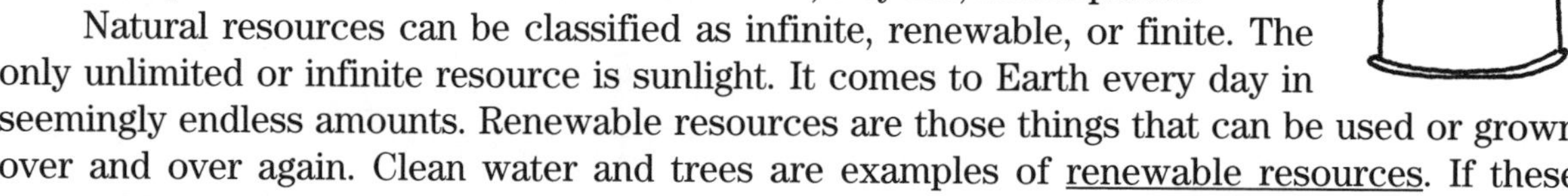

Natural resources can be classified as infinite, renewable, or finite. The only unlimited or infinite resource is sunlight. It comes to Earth every day in seemingly endless amounts. Renewable resources are those things that can be used or grown over and over again. Clean water and trees are examples of renewable resources. If these renewable resources are carefully managed, they should never run out.

Metals and fossil fuels are finite resources. There is only a certain amount of each of these resources on the earth. When they run out, people will have to use something else or do without. Many finite resources can be recycled, like aluminum soda cans. This will help these valuable resources last much longer.

Below, list as many natural resources as you can. Compare lists with at least two other people. Add to your list if you wish.

____

____

____

____

____

____

YOU are a natural resource!

Name ____________________

EARTH'S RESOURCES, CONTINUED

Describe the resources suggested by each picture. Use the underlined words from the article to help you describe them.

Draw a picture and explain how you can use less of one of each kind of resource.

RENEWABLE RESOURCE

FINITE RESOURCE

Name ______________________________

LOOK WHAT I FOUND!

Today you are going to do some scientific research. You will be collecting information or data and recording it. You will need to observe carefully and share your ideas. You will need to think carefully, too. For your observation, you will need this record sheet, a pencil, and a clipboard or other hard surface to write on.

Each group will need:

4 pencils
1 piece of string about 5 feet long
1 ruler
Optional: small digging tool
hand lens

Work with at least two other people. Use your ruler to measure a 12″ square on the ground and poke a pencil into the ground to mark each corner. Wrap your string around the pencils and tie it to mark the boundaries of your square. The earth inside this square is your study site.

Describe your study site. Where is it? What buildings, trees, ponds, etc., are nearby? Is it sunny? Shady? Wet? Is your site on a hill? In a park? Be as specific as you can. Compare your description with others in your group. Add to your description if you wish.

____

____

____

____

____

____

____

____

LOOK WHAT I FOUND!, CONTINUED

Name______________________________

Others in my group ____________________

____

____

Does your site show any signs of erosion?

Stand over your study site and look down on it. Describe what you see. Be as specific as you can.

____

____

____

____

Stoop close to your study site. Get really close. Use a hand lens if possible. Describe what you see.

____

____

____

____

Use your ruler or digging tool and carefully lift some of the soil. Look carefully and use a hand lens if possible. Describe what you see. Be sure to replace the soil or sod when you are finished.

____

____

____

____

Share your observations with others in your group. Add to your record if you wish.

Now compare your findings with another group. Discuss the findings that your two sites have in common and the differences you found. On the back of this sheet, explain how the two sites compare. Explain what you think caused the similarities and differences.

Name ______________________________

YOUR CORNER OF THE WORLD

Your place on the earth is unique. Answer the questions below about your special corner of the world. You may need to use a local map to help you.

1. What is the name of your city or town? If you don't live in a city or town, name the nearest one.

   ____

2. What is the name of the closest river to your home?

   ____

   Into what body of water does your river flow? ______________________________

3. What ocean is nearest your home? _________________________ How far away from you is it? ________________________________

4. What mountain or range of mountains is nearest your home? ______________________

   Can you see any mountains or hills from your home? ______________________________

5. What is the name of the lake nearest your home? ____________________ What do people use this lake for? ____

   ____

   ____

   ____

6. What types of plants grow within walking distance of your home? __________________

   ____

   ____

On the back of this paper, draw a picture or map showing the special features of your corner of the world.

Name________________________________

ONE CONTINENT?

In 1923 Alfred Megener proposed a new scientific theory. He claimed that the continents of today were once one giant land mass—a super continent! It took 50 years to convince other scientists that he was on to something.

Megener's theory has become the study of plate tectonics. Much evidence supports this theory. Identical species of snakes, lizards, and turtles are found in Africa and South America. A deep canyon in the Mid-Atlantic ridges shows that the ocean floors slowly move outward toward the continents. Rock formations in Africa match ones found in Brazil—exactly! See what other evidence you can find to support the theory of Alfred Megener.

Use the underlined words in the paragraph above to solve the puzzle below. Use the numbered letters in each correct answer to fill the boxes and name the super continent.

1. Alfred __ __ ☐ __ __ __ __ proposed a new theory in 1923.
2. All of the __ __ __ __ __ __ __ ☐ __ __ were once one giant land mass.
3. ☐ __ __ __ __ tectonics is the study of the Earth's moving crust.
4. The Mid-__ __ __ ☐ __ __ __ __ ridge has a deep canyon.
5. The __ __ __ ☐ __ floor moves outward from the center toward the continents.
6. Much __ __ __ __ ☐ __ __ __ supports Megener's theory.
7. Rock layers in Brazil match those found in __ __ __ __ __ ☐.

Alfred Megener called the giant land mass that became today's continents...

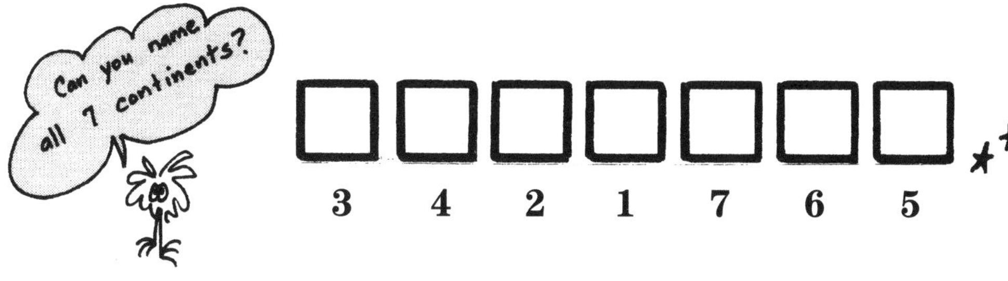

Name ______________________________

COORDINATE THE COORDINATES

Complete the sampler by coloring the squares as shown below.

A-1, A-2, A-3, A-6, A-9, A-10, A-13, A-14, A-15, A-17, A-19, B-1, B-5, B-7, B-9, B-11, B-14, B-17, B-19, C-1, C-2, C-3, C-5, C-6, C-7, C-9, C-10, C-14, C-17, C-18, C-19, D-1, D-5, D-7, D-9, D-14, D-17, D-19, E-1, E-2, E-3, E-5, E-7, E-9,E-11, E-14, E-17, E-19, F-1, F-2, F-3, F-5, F-7, F-9, F-11, F-14, F-17, F-19

A-5

D-10

A-7, A-11, D-11

C-11

LAND QUICK CHECK

Use the word box to help you complete the sentences.

environment	igneous	sedimentary	planet	humus
finite	metamorphic	renewable	magma	erosion

1. Natural resources are the things on our ____________________ that support life.
2. Molten rock or ____________________ pushes up from the mantle of the earth.
3. ____________________, ____________________, and ____________________ are three kinds of rock.
4. Fossil fuels and metals are ____________________ resources.
5. Resources that can be used over or regrown are called ____________________ resources.
6. Our ____________________ is made up of all the things that surround us, both natural and man-made.
7. The surface of the earth is worn down by ____________________.

Write "YES" for true and "NO" for not true.

8. ______ The earth is the largest known planet in our solar system.
9. ______ Many planets have all the things necessary to support life.
10. ______ Australia, Europe, Arctica, Africa, Asia, America, and Antarctica are the seven continents.
11. ______ Land is built up by pressures deep inside the earth.
12. ______ All of the different kinds of rock are formed in much the same way.
13. ______ Silt, clay, and gravel are the three major types of soil.
14. ______ Next to air, dirt or soil is the most common thing found on the earth.

You can tell about more than one thing.

Think about the most interesting or important thing you have learned about the earth's land. Write about it on the back of this sheet.

Name ____________________________

A WATER WORD SEARCH

Circle each of the words you find in the word search. The words can be found either down or across.

Name________________________________

WATER HANDWRITING

watershed ______________________

____

ground water ____________________

____

aquifer _________________________

____

saturation ______________________

____

wetlands _______________________

____

filter ___________________________

____

purification ______________________

____

ice crystal _______________________

____

liquid ___________________________

____

water vapor ______________________

____

Name ______________________________

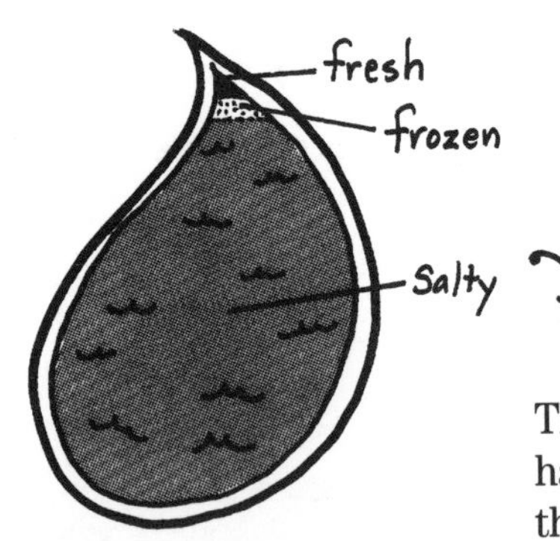

WHERE IS ALL THE WATER?

As you read this story, circle the correct word in each numbered box at the bottom of this sheet.

The earth is a water planet. It is the only 1.__________ known to have liquid water. This makes our earth very special. All living things need water. A tree needs 2.________ and so does a puppy. The tiniest insect and the largest whale need water. People need water, too. In fact, you are about three-fourths water! A 3.__________ could live several weeks without food, but would die in only a few days without water. Without liquid water, Earth would be as 4.__________ as the moon or Mars.

There is no new water. The water you brushed your teeth with this morning has been part of the earth for billions of 5.__________. The same water that is part of you may once have been part of an arctic glacier, a prehistoric forest, or even a dinosaur. Water is constantly being 6.________ and reused again and again.

Water 7.__________ about three-fourths of the earth. On a globe you can see how the continents are really very large islands in the world's oceans. Of all the water on the earth 97% is salty. 8.________ water fills the oceans and seas of the world. About 2% of all Earth's water is frozen in the polar ice caps, glaciers, and icebergs. Only about 1% of all the water on the earth is fresh and liquid. Nearly all the fresh 9.__________ we use comes from rivers, lakes, and ground water.

but
use
pov

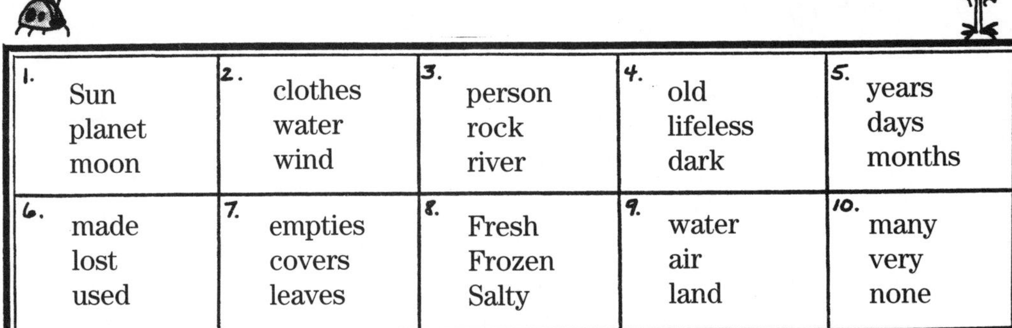

1.	2.	3.	4.	5.
Sun planet moon	clothes water wind	person rock river	old lifeless dark	years days months
6.	**7.**	**8.**	**9.**	**10.**
made lost used	empties covers leaves	Fresh Frozen Salty	water air land	many very none

Name____________________________________

FOOD FROM THE SEA

As you read this story, circle the correct word in each numbered box at the bottom of this sheet.

The oceans and seas have been sources of food for thousands of years. Today nearly 85,000,000 tons of fish are harvested each year. About 6 million 1.__________ make their living in the fishing industry.

Early people used spears, hooks, and crude traps to 2.________ fish. We have become very clever at catching fish. We use electricity to stun them and bright lights to attract 3._________. Fish are harvested in huge nets and processed on huge factory ships. Food from the sea is 4.________ and healthy. Fish is high in protein. Protein is a very 5.__________ nutrient for strong bodies. Seafood is also a good source of vitamins A and D.

Every country with a sea coast 6.__________ fish. Different areas of the world use different types of 7.__________ and different ways to prepare them. In Japan raw tuna is eaten as "sashimi." In Norway herring is 8.__________ with vinegar and spices to make "pickled herring." You have probably eaten cod that has been shaped and breaded to form "fish sticks." There are 30,000 different types of edible fish!

We have gotten so good at taking fish from the 9.__________ that many areas of the oceans have been over fished. Scientists are studying the world's fisheries. Quotas, or limits, have been placed on many types of fish.

10.__________ are needed to protect the remaining fish. Laws also limit the ways fish can be caught. For example, nets must have holes, called mesh, large enough for baby fish to escape. Many countries are working very hard to protect their fisheries.

1. fish people ocean	2. catch cook eat	3. they them this	4. dry dirty tasty	5. bad empty important
6. harvests oceans vitamins	7. fish seas oceans	8. cured caught wasted	9. air sea country	10. Fisheries Quotas Harvests

Name ______________________________

THE WATER CYCLE

Each year the Sun evaporates enough water to cover the entire earth 3½ ft. deep!

Long ago people believed that rivers flowed under the ground from the ocean to the mountains. This is how they thought that the rivers were able to keep flowing. Today we know this is not true. Water does flow from the oceans to the mountains, but not underground. Water flows through the air. You have seen water do this! Clouds are droplets of water flowing through the air. They are part of the earth's hydrological cycle.

All the water that was ever on the earth, or ever will be, is here today. Water changes form, but it is always the same water. The water you washed with this morning may have been flowing down the Nile river last year. The same water may have been part of a dinosaur millions of years ago.

The hydrological or water cycle is the natural system that distributes water over the surface of the earth. Two forces keep the water cycle moving. These forces are heat from the sun and gravity. The heat from the sun causes liquid water to evaporate or change form into water vapor. Later, gravity causes the condensed water to fall back to earth.

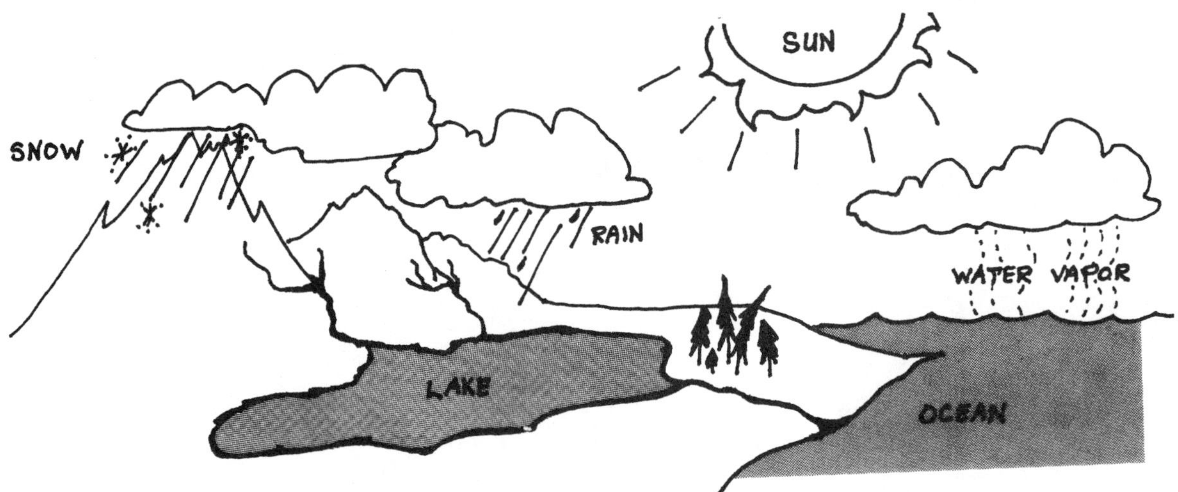

As the sun warms the oceans and the land, water evaporates into the air as water vapor. The invisible water vapor rises and becomes colder. As it cools the vapor forms droplets. These droplets form clouds. Winds move the clouds through the atmosphere. When clouds become colder and more droplets condense, the water collects into heavier drops. The pull of gravity causes precipitation. Water falls to earth as rain. If the air around the cloud is very cold, the droplets form ice crystals and become snow.

Name________________________________

THE WATER CYCLE, CONTINUED

More than three-fourths of all precipitation falls on the ocean. The rest falls on the land. Some water soaks into the ground to become ground water. Some is evaporated back into the air or taken in by plants. Most of the water runs off in streams and rivers. Gravity moves the water down riverbeds and back to the ocean.

The water cycle also explains why river water is fresh while ocean water is salty. When water evaporates from the ocean only the water molecules form water vapor. The salt does not evaporate. The precipitation that feeds rivers is fresh—not salty! Without constant circulation of fresh water, people and other creatures could not live on earth.

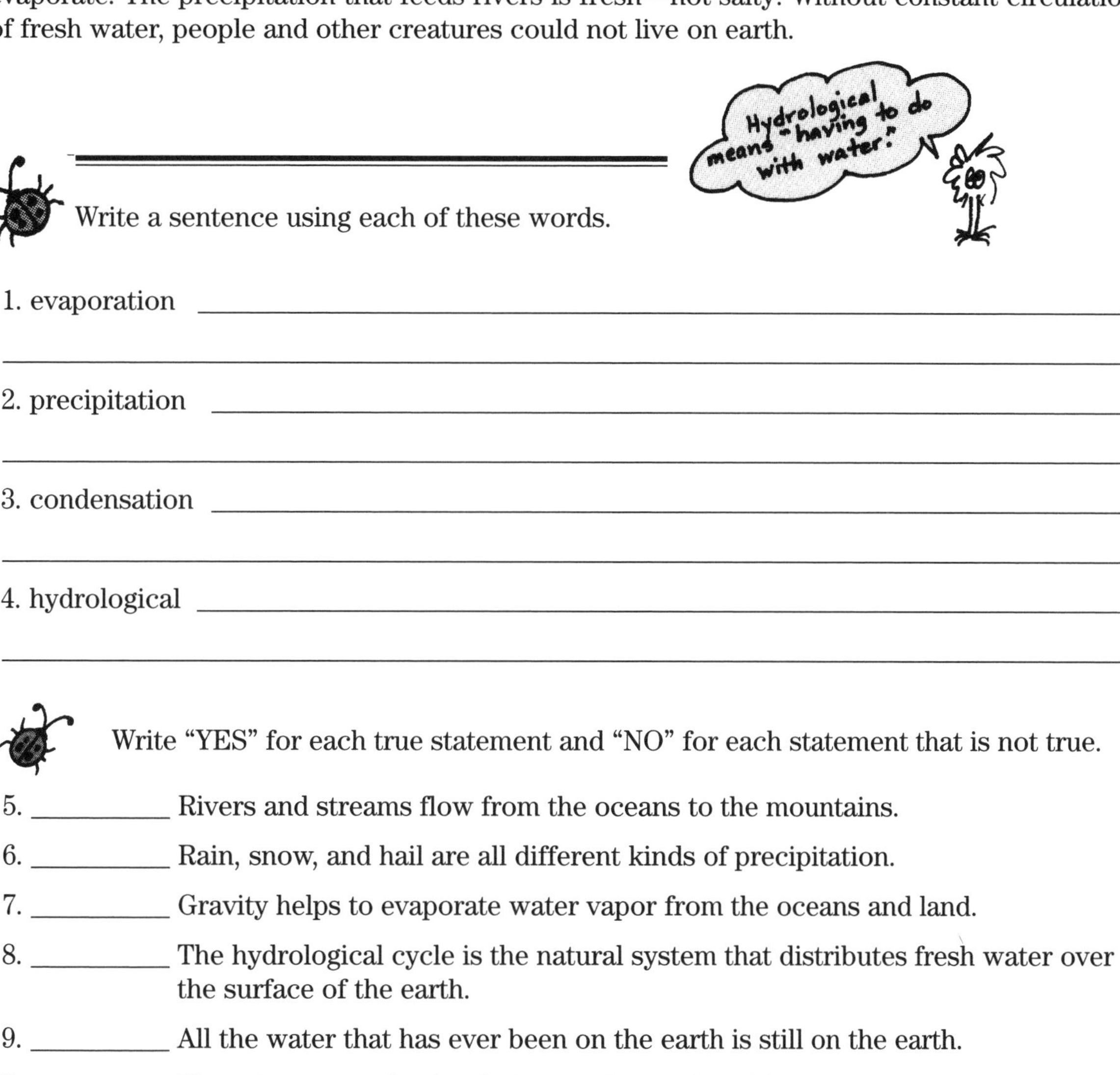

Write a sentence using each of these words.

1. evaporation ____

2. precipitation ____

3. condensation ____

4. hydrological ____

Write "YES" for each true statement and "NO" for each statement that is not true.

5. __________ Rivers and streams flow from the oceans to the mountains.
6. __________ Rain, snow, and hail are all different kinds of precipitation.
7. __________ Gravity helps to evaporate water vapor from the oceans and land.
8. __________ The hydrological cycle is the natural system that distributes fresh water over the surface of the earth.
9. __________ All the water that has ever been on the earth is still on the earth.
10. __________ Water is constantly circulating on the earth and being used over and over.

★ On the back of this page write a paragraph about how the water cycle works.

Name ______________________________

HOW WE USE WATER

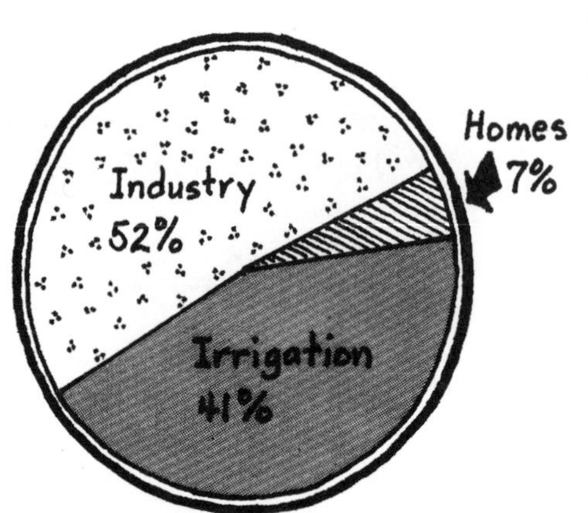

All life processes need water. Every part in your body uses water to take in food for energy and carry away waste. All life on Earth needs water in this way, but people use much more water than is needed for their life processes. People take water from the environment for a variety of uses. Sometimes the water is put back to be reused. Sometimes the water is used up and can't be gathered again for other human uses.

More water is used by industry than for any other human use. About 52% of all the water used by people is used to produce things. Much of the water used by factories is used for cooling. Some is used for cleaning. Cooling and cleaning water can be reused. A small amount of water is used as raw material. This water is made into products like soda.

Almost as much water as factories use is used for irrigation. In many places crops need more water to grow than comes from the rain in that area. Farmers irrigate to give their crops the extra water they need to grow well. About 41% of all the water we use goes to irrigate croplands. Irrigation water is not reusable. Nearly all irrigation water goes back into the atmosphere through evaporation or transpiration.

The water we use in our homes amounts to about 7% of all the water used by people. At home we use water to cook, clean, drink, and flush away wastes. The average person uses about 100 gallons of water every day. Nearly all of the water we use at home is reusable. It goes down the drain and to a treatment plant. Here it is cleaned and put back into the environment. In the summer we use about one-third more water than the rest of the year. This water is sprinkled on about 10 million acres of lawn!

We use water in many other ways without taking it out of the environment. We use it right where it is. The earth's water bodies are a major source of food. More than 85 million tons of food are harvested from the oceans, lakes, and rivers each year.

Name ______________________________

HOW WE USE WATER, CONTINUED

We also depend on these waterways for transportation. Shipping is an important industry in many great cities. Check to see if there is a port near where you live.

We use water for energy. In many area hydro-power is an important source of electricity. Huge dams generate power from the falling water of major rivers. Still another way people use water is for recreation. We love to swim, boat, or just play in and around water.

IT TAKES...

- 5 gallons to flush
- 40 gallons to bathe
- 25 gallons for a 5-minute shower
- 12 gallons to run an automatic dishwasher
- 30 gallons to wash a load of clothes

Write "YES" for each true statement. Write "NO" if it is not true.

1. _____ Industry uses more water than all other human uses.
2. _____ Irrigation water goes back into the environment through evaporation and transpiration.
3. _____ Animals, plants, and people all need water for their life processes.
4. _____ People only use water that is taken out of the environment.
5. _____ Some water that people use can be reused and some is lost back into the atmosphere.

Fill in each blank with a word from the article to complete each sentence.

6. A small amount of the water used by industry is used as raw ______________________.
7. Farmers __________________ to give their crops the extra water they need to grow well.
8. The water we use in our ____________________ amounts to about 7% of all the water used by people.
9. More than 85 ______________________________ tons of food are harvested from the oceans, lakes, and rivers each year.
10. In many areas people depend on hydro-power to generate ________________________.

Tell two interesting things that you learned about how we use water. _____________

____

____

____

Name ________________________________

TURN ON THE WATER

coagulation
filtration
disinfection
aquifer
reservoir
alum
chlorine
impurities
purify
flocs

1. A word that rhymes with "socks" is ____________.

2. A ____________ is a place where water is stored for later use.

3. What three words have the same ending? ______________ ______________ ______________

4. Water is treated to take out ______________.

5. ______________ means "to make clean."

6. ______________ is a shorter name for aluminum sulfate.

When you turned on your faucet this morning to brush your teeth, chances are that clean, clear water flowed out. People expect clear, clean, good-tasting water—and quite a lot of it. Where does all the water we use come from and how does it get into our faucets?

Communities get water from two sources. The first is surface water. Lakes and rivers are sources of surface water. Sometimes communities will build dams across rivers to create lakes or reservoirs for their water supplies. Other cities pump water directly from rivers or natural lakes. Most large cities draw their water from surface water sources.

Another source of fresh water is ground water. Water soaks into the ground and fills the little spaces between grains of sand and rocks. The water sinks into the ground until it meets a water-tight layer under the surface. The water collects above this layer and forms a kind of underground lake called a saturation zone or aquifer. The top of this saturation zone is called the water table. A well drilled into the aquifer will fill with water up to the water table. Many communities, especially smaller ones, pump their water from wells.

Name ____________________________________

Raw Water
Chlorine
Clean Water
1. Coagulation
2. filtration
3. disinfection

TURN ON THE WATER, CONTINUED

The water taken from lakes, rivers, or ground water isn't often clean or clear. You probably wouldn't want to brush your teeth with it. Impurities like dirt, leaves, and germs are common in raw water. That is why communities purify water before it comes to your home.

Most cities treat water in three ways. The first treatment is coagulation. Raw water is pumped into a large mixing tank and a chemical called alum is added. The alum forms sticky globs called flocs. The dirt and other impurities stick to the flocs. Later, in a settling tank, the flocs settle to the bottom and the clearer water is pumped from the top.

The next process is filtration. Water is filtered through sand and gravel. This takes away finer impurities and even some disease germs. Although the filtered water is very clear, it is still not really clean. The third step in water treatment is disinfection. A chemical—chlorine—is added to the water to kill any remaining germs and bacteria.

Water from the treatment plant is stored in tanks, towers, or reservoirs. From storage it is pumped through large pipes called water mains. Smaller pipes connect water mains with each home or business. Water pressure pushes the water through pipes in the walls of your home and right to your faucet. You turn it on and have clean water to brush your teeth.

1. Two sources of water for communities is ______________ water and ________________ water.

2. Water taken directly from rivers, lakes, and ground water is clean and clear. (YES, NO)

3. ________________ is a chemical added to water for disinfection.

4. The top level of the saturation zone or aquifer is called the ______________.

5. What does water pressure do? ____

____

6. Coagulation removes (dirt, germs, chlorine) from the raw water.

Name ______________________________

DOWN THE DRAIN

1. Water that has been used for cleaning, cooking, or flushing is called ______________________________.
2. ______________________________ are bits of food, body waste, or dirt in raw sewage.
3. Dishwashers and flush toilets are ______________________ of modern life.
4. ______________________________ is left on the bottom of a sedimentation tank.
5. Third and ______________________________ mean about the same.
6. ______________________________ is the liquid left after sewage has been treated.

conveniences
waste water
Contaminates
sedimentation
Sludge
Effluent
appliances
particles
chlorine
tertiary

One hundred years ago few people had any plumbing inside their homes. There were no appliances to use water and no toilets that flushed like ours. As more modern conveniences came into homes, more and more water was used—water to clean, cook, and flush. You use about 100 gallons of water every day. Where does the water go when you are finished with it?

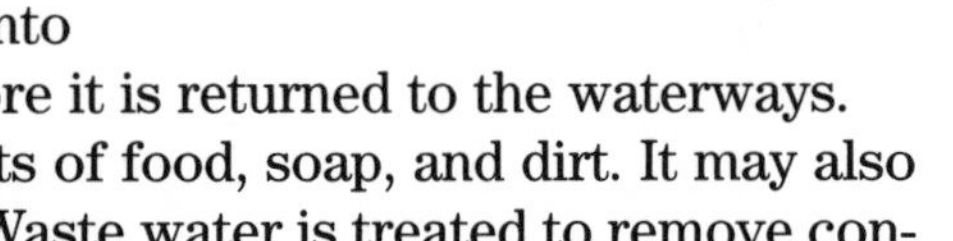

Eventually all water returns to the rivers and oceans. In many parts of the world waste water is simply dumped into rivers. In North America most waste water is treated before it is returned to the waterways.

Raw sewage or waste water contains body waste, bits of food, soap, and dirt. It may also contain harmful chemicals and disease-causing bacteria. Waste water is treated to remove contaminates and make the water clean before it is returned to the rivers or oceans.

Most sewage is treated by central sewerage systems. Sewage is piped from homes and businesses to a central treatment plant. Here it may be treated in one, two, or three steps.

The first or primary step screens the raw sewage to take our large items, such as food scraps. Then a grit chamber settles out fine particles like sand. A sedimentation tank lets solids sink to the bottom. These solids form a thick black sludge. Also in the sedimentation tank, oil and grease float to the top of the tank. The grease and oil are skimmed off the liquid. The liquid pumped from the sedimentation tank is called effluent. If the effluent is not going to be treated further, chlorine is added to kill harmful bacteria.

Name________________________________

DOWN THE DRAIN, CONTINUED

In the secondary treatment step, helpful bacteria and oxygen help to break down harmful chemicals in the sludge. Treated sludge can be used as fertilizer or disposed of in sanitary landfills. The effluent is trickled over crushed rock covered with helpful bacteria. After this treatment, the effluent is usually returned to a river or ocean.

Tertiary or third stage treatment is not used very often. It is expensive and rarely necessary. Tertiary treatment uses chemicals and microscopic screens. Effluent from tertiary treatment is suitable for use by industry and even for drinking.

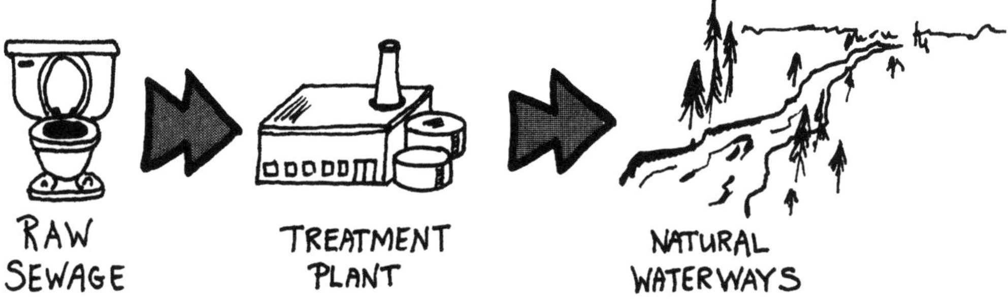

1. You use about 100 gallons of water every day. (YES, NO)

2. What are three things raw sewage contains? ______________________________

____

3. Raw sewage or waste water is (50%, 78%, 99%) water.

4. Why is chlorine added to some effluent? ______________________________

____

5. What is the thick black sediment at the bottom of primary treatment tanks? __________

____

6. What floats to the top of the effluent in the sedimentation tank? __________

____

Name ______________________________

HOW DO YOU USE WATER?

Every family is different and their homes are, too. Because families and homes are different, they use water in different ways and in different amounts. Answer these questions about your home and family.

1. How many adults live with you? ________________
2. How many children live in your home? ________________
3. How many faucets are in your house? ________________
4. How many toilets are in your house? ________________
5. How many bath tubs or showers? ________________
6. Do you have a washing machine? ________________
7. Does your family use a dishwasher? ________________
8. Do you have a lawn or garden to water? ________________

Put your answers to the questions above in the first column below. With a group of 3 or 4 friends, share your answers and fill in the chart below. If you like, add more items to the chart.

Name					
Adults					
Children					
Faucets					
Toilets					
Tubs					
Washer					
Dishwasher					
Lawn					

Name ______________________________

HOW DO YOU USE WATER?, CONTINUED

Discuss the answers on your chart with your group. Discuss the questions below. Write down your own answers. Group members do not have to agree on their answers.

1. Whose family has the most people? ______________________________

2. Which families had a dishwasher? ______________________________

____

3. Which families had lawns or gardens? ______________________________

____

4. Which family do you think uses the most water? ______________________________

   Why do you think this is so? ______________________________

____

____

5. Which family do you think uses the least water? ______________________________

   Why do you think this is so? ______________________________

____

____

6. Do families with more people always use more water than smaller families? __________

   Explain why or why not. ______________________________

____

____

____

7. Discuss other ways people use water. Write down three of your favorites. ______________________________

____

____

____

____

A faucet dripping once each second wastes 880 gallons of water each year!

Name ______________________________

EASY COME, EASY GO?

Each community is unique. Some are huge and some are very small. Communities have different needs, locations, industries, and populations. Your community is not exactly like any other. Answer the questions below about your community. You may not know all of the answers, but you can find out by doing some research. Start by asking your teachers, friends, and family. Who else might know the answers?

1. Where does the water you use in your home come from? ______________________

2. Who is responsible for supplying you with clean drinking water? Is it your city, county, or a water association? ______________________

3. Is your home's water measured by a meter? ____________ If you have a water meter, where is it located and what does it look like? ______________________

4. How much water does your household use in one month? (HINT: Check you family water bill.) ______________________

5. How is the water you use treated before it comes to your home? ______________________

Name____________________________________

EASY COME, EASY GO?, CONTINUED

6. Does your community add fluoride to the water supply? ______________________________

7. How is waste water from your home treated? ____

____

____

8. How is waste water from industry treated in your community? ______________________

____

____

9. Who or what is the largest water user in your community? __________________________

____

10. Where and how is treated waste water returned to the natural environment? _________

____

____

____

In the space below make two drawings. Show how water gets to you and where it goes when you are finished with it.

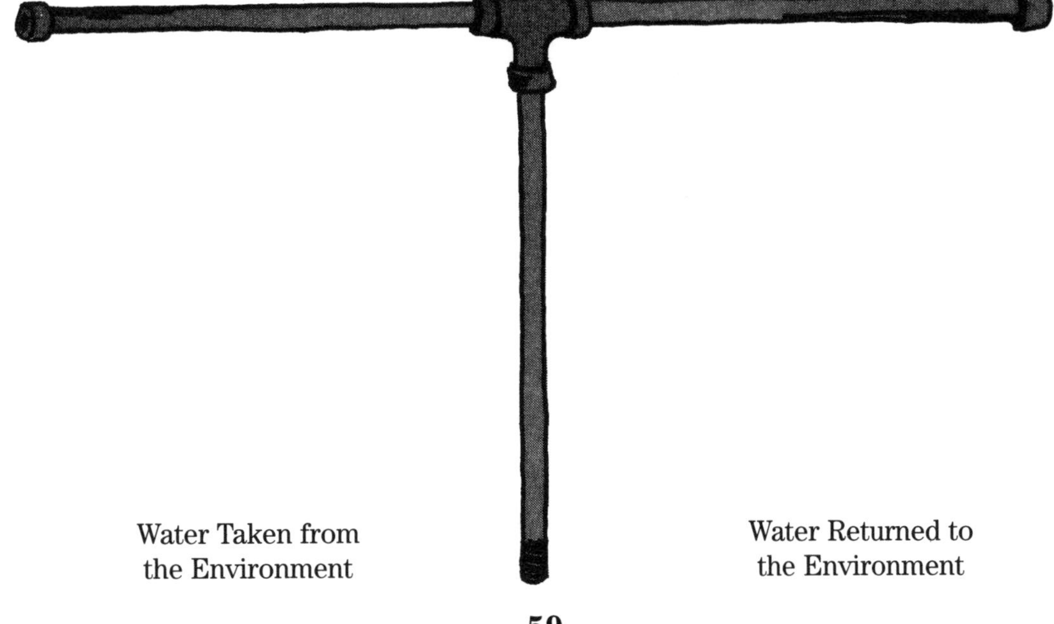

Water Taken from the Environment

Water Returned to the Environment

Name ______________________________

SOLAR PURIFIER

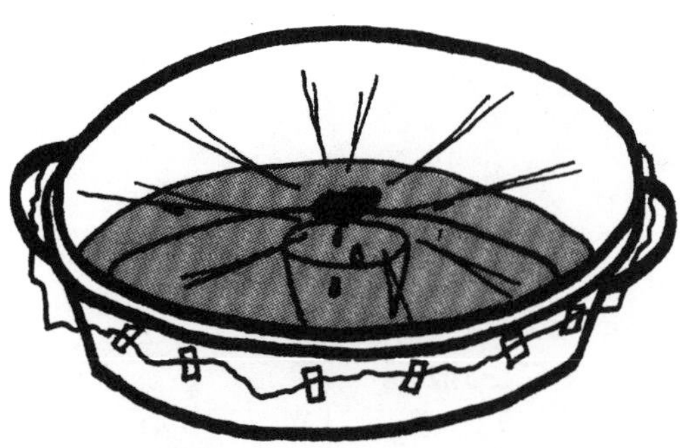

The sun can clean water. You can make a simple water purifier that is powered by solar energy. You will need a large pan, a glass (the sides on the pan must be taller than the glass), a dry cleaning bag, tape, two small clean rocks, and some dirty water. Place the pan where it will be in the sunshine for most of the day. Pour about three inches of muddy water into the pan. Set the glass in the center of the water. If the glass tries to float, put one of the rocks in the bottom of the glass.

Cover the pan with the dry cleaning bag and tape it securely to the sides of the pan. Gently put one of the rocks on the plastic film directly above the glass. Congratulations! You have made a solar water purifier. Now look carefully at your purifier about every hour. Notice what is happening. You may want to write down your observations.

The solar water purifier works by distilling the water. The heat from the sun causes evaporation. Liquid water turns to water vapor. The plastic film is cooler than the air inside the pan. When the water vapor touches the plastic, the water vapor turns back into liquid water. As the liquid water collects on the plastic, it runs down and drips into the glass.

Number the directions in the correct order.

_____ Pour three inches of muddy water into the pan.

_____ Cover the pan with plastic film.

_____ Put the pan in a sunny location.

_____ Put a small rock on the plastic above the glass.

_____ Tape the plastic securely to the sides of the pan.

_____ Set the glass in the center of the pan.

Distillation is one way to change salt water into fresh water.

Write a paragraph telling how a solar water purifier works. ______________________

____

____

____

____

Name____________________________________

WATER USE MATH

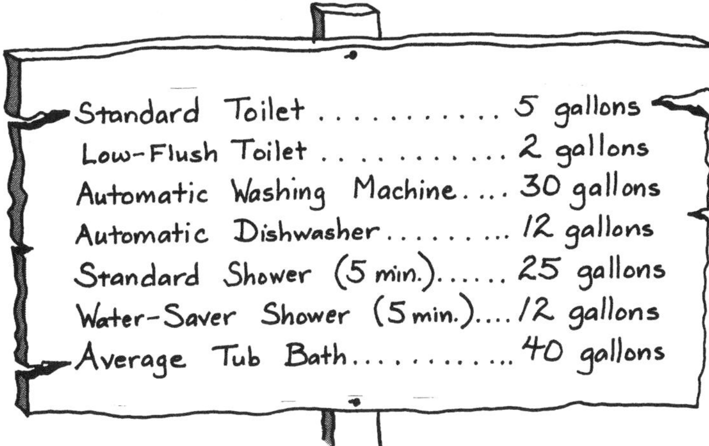

 Solve the problems.

WORK AREA

1. Your family replaces your regular toilet with a low-flush toilet. How much water will you save each time you flush?__________________ How much will you save each day if your family flushes ten times a day? __________________ How much water would you save in a week?__________________

2. You dad takes a bath every day. You convince him to take a 5-minute standard shower instead. How much water is saved? __________________ How much water will be saved in one week? __________________

3. You help your mom replace your standard shower with a water-saver shower head. How much less water will you use for a 5-minute shower now?__________________

4. On Saturday you help sort five loads of laundry. How much water will be needed to clean all of the clothes? __________________

5. Your grandma runs her dishwasher every day. How much water will be used in one week?__________________ If she only runs full loads, she will use her dishwasher only four times each week. How much water does four loads use?__________________ How much water would your grandma save? __________________

 Write a word problem on the back of this paper. Use the information above about water use. Give it to someone else to solve. Check the person's answer.

Name ______________________________

CLUES: Use the list of words at the bottom to help you fill in each blank. The letter in the box in each answer fits into the puzzle above. The first one is done for you.

1. A place to store water is called a R E S [E] R V O I R.
2. All of the things that surround us are parts of our __ __ [ ] __ __ __ __ __ __ __ __ __.
3. __ [ ] __ __ __ __ __ __ __ __ is the point when something, like a sponge, is holding as much water as possible.
4. Any dirt, germs, or other things that need to be removed to make water clean are __ __ [ ] __ __ __ __ __ __ __ __.
5. Chlorine is added to water for __ __ __ __ __ __ __ __ __ __ __ [ ] __.
6. Farmers use __ __ [ ] __ __ __ __ __ __ __ __ to give their crops extra water to grow.
7. An [ ] __ __ __ __ __ __ __ is another name for the saturation zone of ground water.
8. __ __ __ __ __ __ [ ] __ __ uses more water than all other human uses.
9. Alum is added to raw water to form sticky globs called flocs in a process called __ __ __ __ __ __ [ ] __ __ __ __ __ __.
10. __ __ __ __ __ __ __ __ __ [ ] __ is a treatment process where water is filtered through sand and gravel to remove impurities.
11. Rain, snow, and hail are all __ __ __ __ __ __ __ __ __ __ __ __ __ [ ].

IRRIGATION	ENVIRONMENT	INDUSTRY	AQUIFER	PRECIPITATION
SATURATION	DISINFECTION	IMPURITIES	FILTRATION	COAGULATION

Name___________________________________

WATER QUICK CHECK

Use the word box to help you complete the sentences.

precipitation	sewage	evaporation	sludge	quotas
purified	reservoir	irrigation	effluent	industry

1. Raw water is _______________ to remove impurities and make it safe to drink.
2. A _______________ is where water is stored for future use.
3. Raw _______________ contains body waste, bits of food, soap, dirt, chemicals, and bacteria.
4. _______________ is the liquid left after sewage is treated.
5. Limits on the amount of fish harvested are called _______________ .
6. _______________ is when liquid water changes to a gas.
7. More water is used by _______________ than any other human use.

Write "YES" for true and "NO" for not true.

8. _______ You could live several weeks without food, but only a few days without water.
9. _______ Water covers about one-half of the earth's surface.
10. _______ New water is added to the water cycle every time it rains.
11. _______ Water taken from rivers and lakes is usually clean and clear.
12. _______ The oceans and seas are an important food source.
13. _______ All life processes need water.
14. _______ It is safe to return waste water directly to the ocean.

★ Think about the most interesting or important thing you have learned about water. Write about it on the back of this sheet.

Name ______________________________

AN AIR WORD SEARCH

Circle each of the words you find in the word search. The words can be found either down or across.

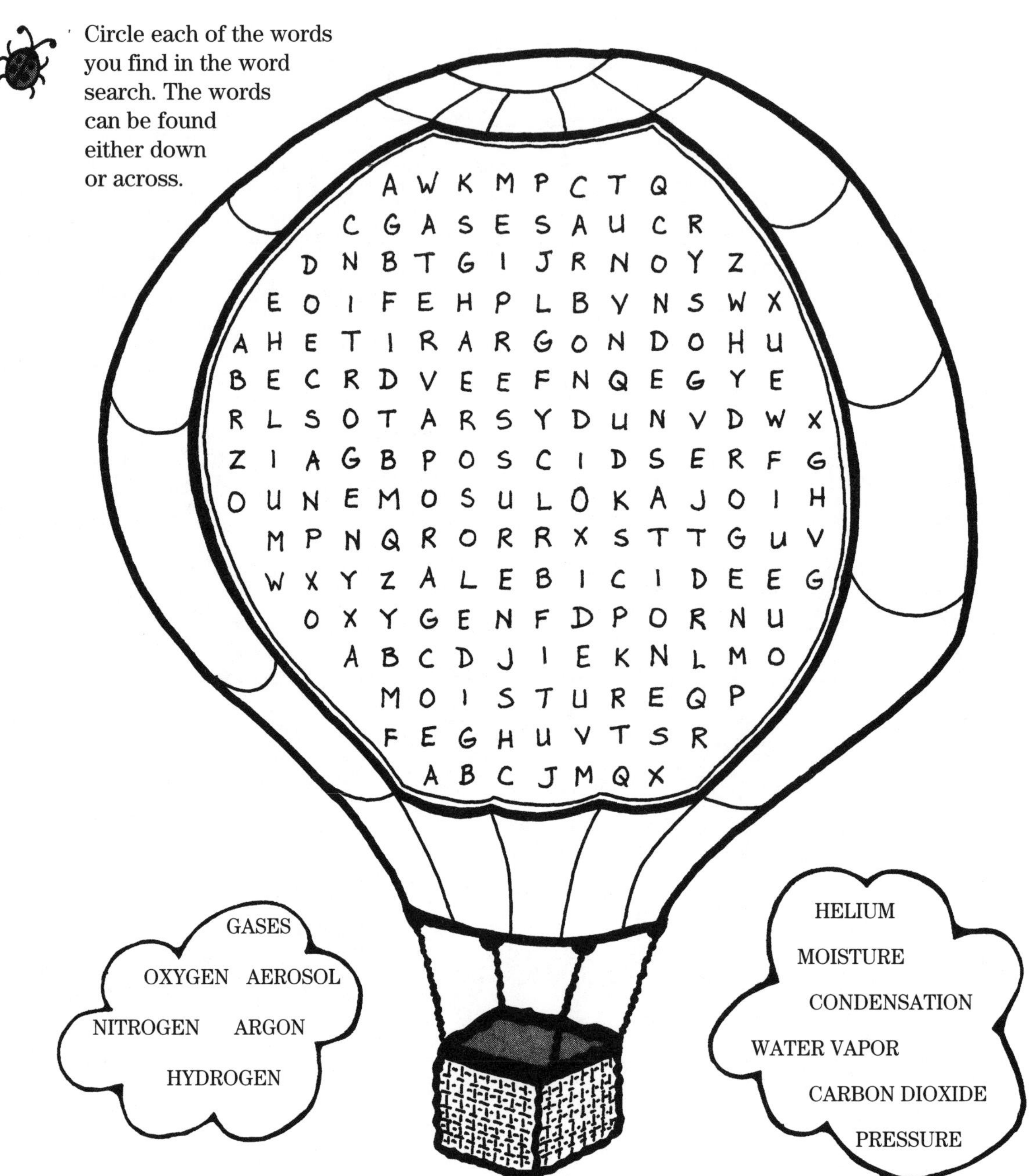

Name ______________________________

AIR HANDWRITING

atmosphere ______________________________

____

troposphere ______________________________

____

stratosphere ______________________________

____

mesosphere ______________________________

____

thermosphere ______________________________

____

ozone ______________________________

____

ultraviolet ______________________________

____

meteor ______________________________

____

greenhouse ______________________________

____

meteorologist ______________________________

____

Name ________________________________

I NEED SOME AIR

As you read this story, circle the correct word in each numbered box at the bottom of this sheet.

Our earth is surrounded by a blanket that is 600 miles thick. The 1.__________ is our atmosphere. Without this special mixture of gases, Earth would be a lifeless 2.__________. Plants, animals, and people all depend on the air for life.

Your body needs a constant supply of 3.__________. You could probably live a month without food. Without water you might 4.__________ for a week. If you had no air you could live only a few minutes. You breathe about 2,750 gallons of air every day!

The atmosphere keeps the 5.__________ surface a comfortable temperature. Layers in the atmosphere trap the sun's heat and keeps it from 6.____________ at night. The atmosphere deflects excess heat during the day. Without our atmosphere the 7.____________ on the earth's surface could reach 300 degrees or more.

Our atmosphere acts as a shield. It protects the 8.__________ from the sun's harmful rays. Ultraviolet rays from the sun can damage both plants 9.___________ animals. The ozone layer of the atmosphere absorbs these 10.__________ rays. The atmosphere also protects us from objects from space hitting the earth.

1.	2.	3.	4.	5.
earth blanket mile	planet moon sun	plants air animals	need live depend	earth's sun's moon's
6.	**7.**	**8.**	**9.**	**10.**
escaping trapping adding	surfaces atmospheres temperatures	moon sun earth	or with and	helpful comfortable harmful

IN THE AIR

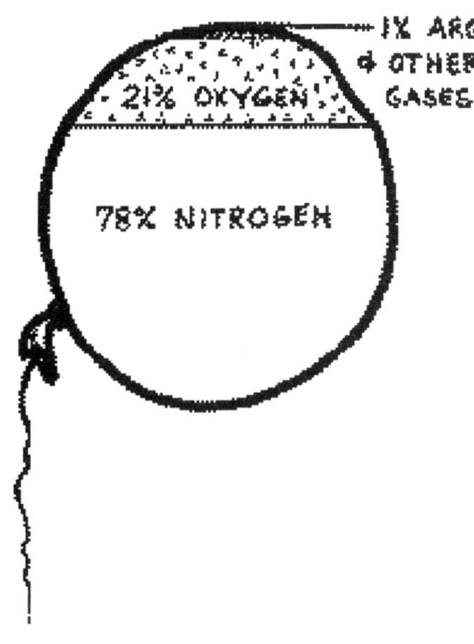

As you read this story, circle the correct word in each numbered box at the bottom of this sheet.

You breathe in and out about 20 times every minute. Do you know what you are breathing? Air is a mixture of gases, water vapor, 1._______ dust.

Most of the gas in the 2.___________ is nitrogen. Nitrogen makes up about 78% of dry air. Oxygen is the next most common 3.__________. About 21% of the air is 4.__________. That leaves only about 1% of the air. This 1% is mostly argon gas with a bit of carbon dioxide and several other 5.____________.

The amount and kinds of gases in the air are about the same everywhere. The amount of water vapor in the air varies with 6.____________ and place. Humidity is how much 7.__________ vapor is in the air. The more water vapor that is in the air, the higher the humidity. Warm air can hold more water 8.______________ than cool air. Most weather reports list the air's relative 9.________________.

The air also contains tiny bits of solid materials. These bits are called aerosols. Dust, pollen, salts, and ash are all 10.__________. The amount of aerosols in the air varies from place to place. Smoke and industrial pollution greatly increase aerosols. Rain washes particles from the air. That is why the air smells fresh after a rain.

1.	2.	3.	4.	5.
and or but	air water dirt	gas solid liquid	smoke oxygen vapor	liquids gases solids
6.	**7.**	**8.**	**9.**	**10.**
gases time nitrogen	common gas water	liquid solid vapor	size length humidity	aerosols gases water

Name ______________________________

UP IN THE AIR

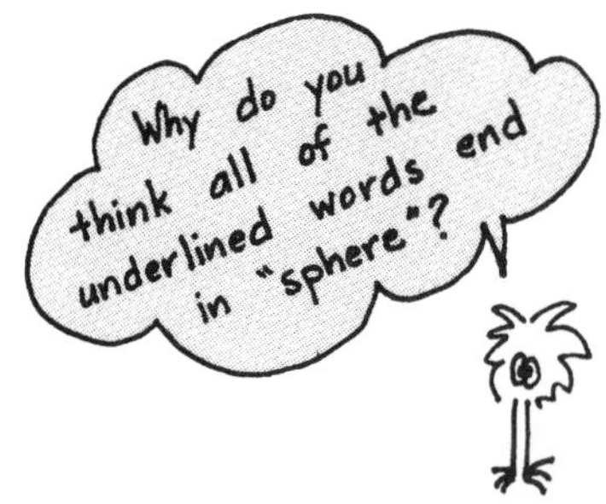

The elements in the air you are breathing are about the same no matter where you live. You are sucking in nitrogen, oxygen, water vapor, and a little dust. Does this mean that all of our atmosphere is the same? As you travel around the surface of the earth, this is true. However, if you travel up, the atmosphere is very different.

Scientists divide the earth's atmosphere into four main parts. The part of the atmosphere you live in is called the troposphere. This layer is only about 6 to 10 miles thick. It is a bit thicker at the equator and thinner at the poles. About 75% of all the earth's air is in the troposphere. There is too little air at the upper limit of the troposphere to support life.

Listen carefully to radio or television weather forecasters. The jet stream they talk about is the top of the troposphere.

Above the troposphere is the stratosphere. This layer of atmosphere extends up about 30 miles. There are little or no weather disturbances in the stratosphere. Airline pilots like to fly in the lower stratosphere because of this smooth air. Have you ever flown in the stratosphere? The top of the stratosphere is the ozone layer. Ozone is an important shield for the earth. Ozone absorbs harmful ultraviolet rays from the sun. These are the rays that cause sunburns.

The mesosphere extends from the stratosphere to about 50 miles above the earth's surface. This layer has very strong winds. These winds blow from east to west in the summer and from west to east in the winter. Have you ever seen a shooting star? That was a meteor burning up in the mesosphere.

The highest layer of our atmosphere is the thermosphere. Only rocket-powered vehicles can fly this high. The thermosphere is mostly hydrogen and helium. Temperatures here can reach 3600° F!

Use the underlined words from the article above to label the numbered spaces in the illustration on the next page.

Name ________________________________

UP IN THE AIR, CONTINUED

Fill in the correct number of miles in the spaces on the right of the illustration below. Draw in and label each of the features listed. Put each one in the correct layer of the atmosphere.

CLOUDS — METEORS

SPACE SHUTTLE  — AIRPLANE

OZONE LAYER  — YOU

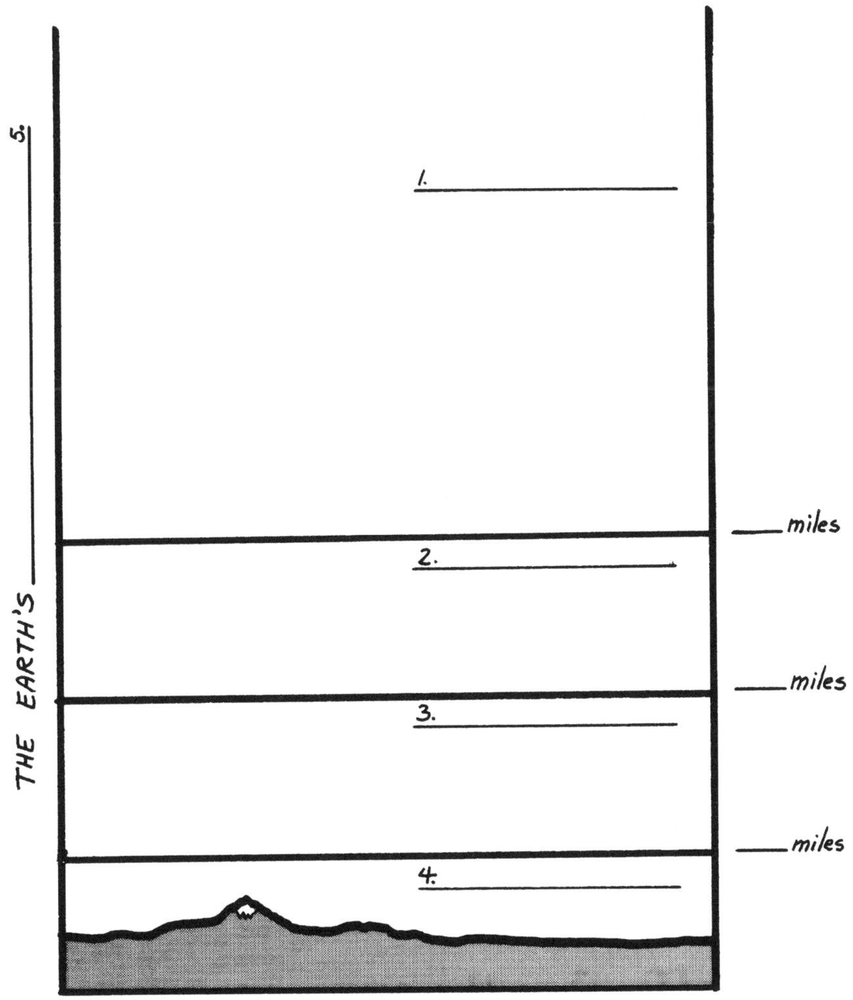

Name ______________________________

WEATHER AND THE ATMOSPHERE

Ready:

- troposphere
- meteorologist
- temperature
- moisture
- moderates
- mass
- vapor
- condensation
- precipitation
- humidity

1. The word that ends like the word "biologist" is ______________________________.
2. The only one-syllable word is ______________________________.
3. A layer of the atmosphere is the ______________________________.
4. ______________________ is a word that rhymes with "paper."
5. A word that has the same "oi" sound as in the word "boil."
   ____
6. ______________________________ is the measure of hot and cold.

Set:

Nearly all weather happens in the troposphere, the layer of the atmosphere nearest the earth. Meteorologists study four main parts or factors in weather. These factors are temperature, air pressure, wind, and moisture.

Temperature is the amount of heat in the air. Air temperature depends on the greenhouse effect. The air inside a car parked in the sun can be much warmer than the air outside the car. The glass in the car's windows lets the sun's heat energy in, but stops it from leaving. The earth's atmosphere acts in much the same way as the car's window glass. The atmosphere traps the heat from the sun and keeps it from being lost back into space. The greenhouse effect moderates the earth's temperature. It keeps the earth's surface from getting too cold or too hot to support life.

Name________________________________

WEATHER AND THE ATMOSPHERE, CONTINUED

Air pressure is the force or weight of the air pressing down on the earth. Air pressure is not the same everywhere. Temperature effects air pressure. Warm air has less pressure than cool air. That is why some homes have ceiling fans. Warmer air rises to the top of a room. A fan is used to push the warm air down where the people are. Warm air masses in the atmosphere have low pressure and are called "lows." Cooler air masses have high pressure and are called "highs."

In the atmosphere air moves from areas of high pressure to areas of low pressure. This makes wind. The bigger the difference in air pressure between two air masses, the stronger the wind will be. Hurricanes occur when two air masses have a very great difference in air pressure. This is most common in tropical areas. Wind is measured in miles or kilometers per hour. Winds are named for the directions from which they flow. A west wind blows from west to east.

Even when it isn't raining, the air is wet. The water vapor in the air is called humidity. Warm air can hold more moisture than cool air. As warm moist air rises and cools, water vapor condenses. Condensation equals precipitation—rain, snow, sleet, or hail.

1. Where does nearly all weather happen? ________________________________

2. ________________ is how much water vapor is in the air.

3. The greenhouse effect keeps moisture in the air to make rain. (YES, NO)

4. What word from the second paragraph means "to keep from getting too hot or too cold"?

   ____

5. Air pressure is (always, not, nearly) the same everywhere on the earth.

6. ____________________ are scientists who study the earth's weather.

Name ________________________________

ATMOSPHERIC PRESSURE

You can't see the air, but you can feel it on your face when the wind blows. On a calm day, you don't really feel the air at all. Even when you can't feel it, air is pushing on you.

The molecules in the air bounce around and bump into each other. They also bump into everything else—including you. Air is pushing down on you with a weight of about 1,000 pounds. You don't crumple because the pressure of the air is the same all around you. Air presses about 15 pounds per square inch. This is called air pressure or atmospheric pressure.

Atmospheric pressure is not the same everywhere on the earth. Altitude affects pressure. The higher above sea level you go, the less pressure. There is less air and, therefore, fewer molecules to bounce around.

Temperature also affects air pressure. Warm air has less pressure than cool air. Meteorologists measure air pressure with a barometer. This is important for predicting the movements of air masses.

The earth's surface heats unequally. The sun heats water more slowly than land areas. The air close to the surface is warmed by the land or water. Air above the oceans heats more slowly than air above the land. Warm air rises because it has lower pressure. Cool air rushes in underneath because its pressure is higher. This is how wind happens. This process is called convection. It is the circulation of air in the atmosphere.

The constant mixing of the air is important. If you live in a low-lying area you may have experienced an air inversion. This is when cool air becomes trapped under a layer of warm air. The trapped air stagnates or remains still. Pollution from cars and industry are trapped near the earth's surface. This can make the air unfit to breathe. Plants, animals, and people suffer. Understanding atmospheric pressure can help predict these inversions. Convection is important to clean the air.

Use the underlined words in this article to help you label the illustration on the next page.

Name________________________________

ATMOSPHERIC PRESSURE, CONTINUED

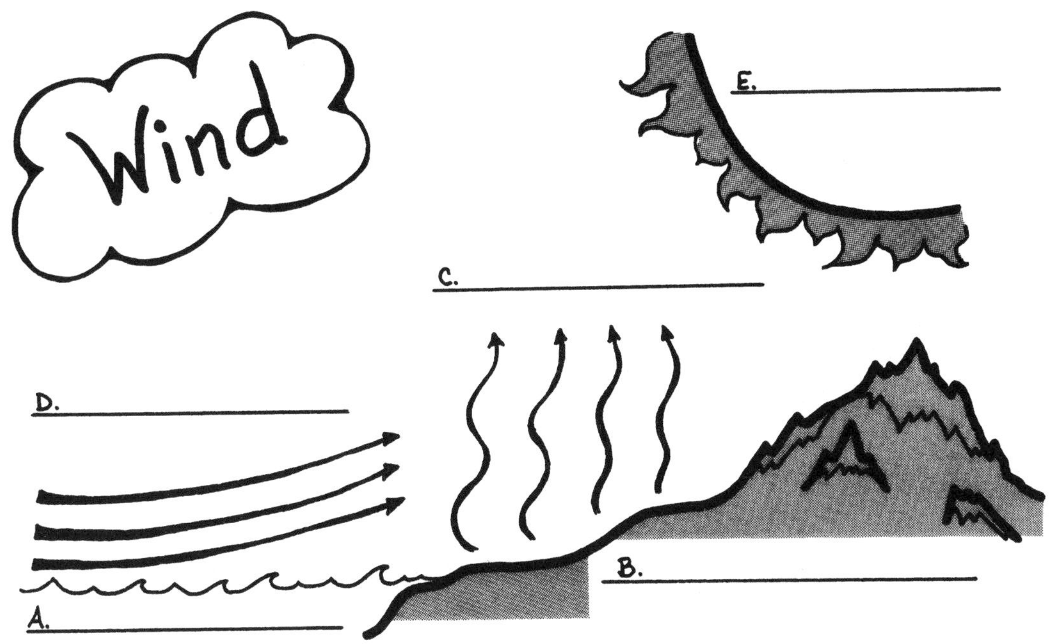

 Circle the best answer for each question. Look back at the article if you need help.

1. Air (molecules, bumps, atmosphere) bounce around and bump into each other.

2. The pressure of the air is (the same, different, too much) all around you.

3. Air presses about (1000, 15, 150) pounds per square inch.

4. Convection is the circulation of (inversions, meteorologists, air) in the atmosphere.

5. An air (pressure, atmosphere, inversion) traps cool air near the earth's surface under a layer of warm air.

 On the back of this sheet, explain how wind happens. Try to use these words in your explanation: air pressure, circulation, and convection. ★

Name ______________________________

OUR CHANGING CLIMATE

Ready:

altitude
unequal
convection
moderate
orbit
tilt
glaciers
absorb
atmosphere
intensity

1. ____________________ is the only one-syllable word on the list.

2. A river of ice that doesn't melt away in summer is called a ____________________.

3. The thin blanket of air surrounding the earth is our ____________________.

4. The higher the ____________________, the further you are above sea level.

5. ____________________ is the opposite of equal.

6. The earth moves around the sun in an ____________________.

Set:

The weather can change very quickly. Meteorologists change their forecasts from hour to hour. Climate is the average of many, many years' weather. Climate changes very slowly. It can take thousands or even millions of years for climate to change.

Some climate changes are caused by the movement of the earth. The earth's orbit slowly changes about every 100,000 years. The tilt of the earth shifts in 40,000-year cycles. Even the intensity of the sun may change over time. Scientists believe that the earth is several billion years old. There have been times in its history when the earth has been much warmer than it is now. At times the earth has been warm enough to melt the polar ice. At other times much of North America and Europe were covered by glaciers.

Climate is controlled by the sun, the oceans, and the earth's atmosphere. Our moon is about the same distance from the sun, but never gets above freezing.

Name________________________________

OUR CHANGING CLIMATE, CONTINUED

Earth is warm because of the atmosphere. The atmosphere traps the sun's heat. The air absorbs some heat directly from the sun. Mostly the air is warmed by the heat from the oceans and land masses. This explains why the air near the earth's surface is warmer than the air at high altitudes.

Climate is not the same everywhere on the earth. The sun's rays strike the earth more directly at the equator than at the poles. This unequal heating causes winds and ocean currents. Wind, rain, and humidity are all parts of this convection or heat transfer.

Land masses and ocean water heat at different rates. On a sunny day, beach sand can be very hot while the ocean waves nearby are cool. Water heats slowly and holds heat longer than land. Areas near large bodies of water often enjoy more moderate temperatures than inland areas. Winds off the water keep the land areas from getting too hot or too cold.

Small changes in climate are important. Even small changes can greatly affect our ability to grow food. Scientists believe that people's activities can change climate by changing the earth's heat balance. Burning fossil fuels releases carbon dioxide that traps more heat in the atmosphere. Particles in the air from industrial pollution may screen out some of the sun rays and cool the earth. Adapting to climate changes may become one of our greatest challenges.

1. ____________________ changes slowly over thousands and millions of years.

2. Glaciers have covered most of North America and Europe. (YES, NO)

3. The (earth, moon, atmosphere) traps heat and holds it near the earth's surface.

4. What three factors control the earth's climate? ____________________________, ________________________, and ______________________________

5. Small changes in climate are important because ____________________________________ ____.

6. Scientists believe that ____________________ activities may be changing the earth's heat balance.

Name ______________________________

AIR PRESSURE CHALLENGE

Today you will be discovering some things about air pressure. You should work with at least two other people. You will have an opportunity to observe and draw conclusions. Share and discuss your conclusions with your group. For your inquiry your group will need:

- record sheets
- wooden slat at least 24″ long
- 2 sheets of newspaper
- hammer
- heavy table

1. Look carefully at the wooden slat and the sheets of newspaper. Which do you think is stronger? ______________________________

   Why do you think this is true? ______________________________

   ____

   ____

   ____

Share your answers with your group and add to your answers if you like.

Follow these directions carefully.

a. Place the wooden slat on the table so that about one-third of the slat is sticking out over the edge of the table.

b. Cover the table top with the newspaper. The two-thirds of the slat that is on the table should be covered. With your hands, smooth the paper flat against the table.

Name________________________________

AIR PRESSURE CHALLENGE, CONTINUED

I worked with:

____

____

____

____

____

2. You are soon going to smack the slat with a hammer. What do you think will happen when you do? ______________________________

____

Why do you think this will happen? ______________________________

____

Use the hammer to sharply smack the slat near the end that is sticking out from the edge of the table.

3. What happened? ______________________________

____

Why do you think this happened? ______________________________

____

Share your ideas with other groups and add to your answers if you like.

Air pressure at sea level is about 15 pounds per square inch. Measure the area of the newspaper in your inquiry. Figure out how many pounds of air were sitting on your newspaper.

Name ______________________________

GREAT MINDS

Many people have contributed to our knowledge of the earth's atmosphere. Each small discovery was a part of the puzzle. Each person of vision added a piece to our understanding. Scientists continue to discover new information about the atmosphere. The people listed below have paved the way for the great minds of the future—maybe a great mind like yours!

Evangelista Torricelli	Galileo
Blaise Pascal	John Jeffries
Aristotle	Joseph-Louis Gay-Lussac
Antoine Lavoisier	Edmond Halley
Sir Francis Beaufort	Benjamin Franklin
Carl W. Scheele	Joseph Priestly
Vilhelm Bjerkness	Lewis Fry Richardson
Gaspard Coriolis	Carl-Gustaf Rossby

Choose three people you would like to know more about from the list above. Write their names in the spaces below.

1.______________________ 2.______________________ 3.______________________

Use the index volume of an encyclopedia to help you locate information about each of the three people you choose. Take notes on a separate sheet for each person. Find out about when and where they lived, and what sort of work they did. Note any interesting facts you find and, especially, their contributions to the study of the atmosphere.

Complete a "A Great Mind" sheet for one of your atmospheric explorers.

A GREAT MIND

★ ________________________________ ★
(name)

by________________________________
(your name)

★ When and where did your Great Mind live? ________________________________
____
____

★ What sort of work did your Great Mind do? ________________________________
____
____

★ What important discovery\contribution did your Great Mind make to the study of the atmosphere? Why was it important? ________________________________
____
____

What was the most interesting fact you found about your Great Mind? ____________
____
____

★★★ In this space draw an illustration that shows something unique about your Great Mind. Choose an illustration that represents the contribution of your atmospheric explorer.

Name ______________________________

HOT OR COLD?

Measure the temperature outside at about the same time every day for 10 days. Record the temperatures below.

DAY 1	________°	DAY 6	________°
DAY 2	________°	DAY 7	________°
DAY 3	________°	DAY 8	________°
DAY 4	________°	DAY 9	________°
DAY 5	________°	DAY 10	________°

Should I get my jacket?

Your teacher will help you to label the temperatures on the left-hand edge of the graph below. Color the bar graph to show the temperature each day.

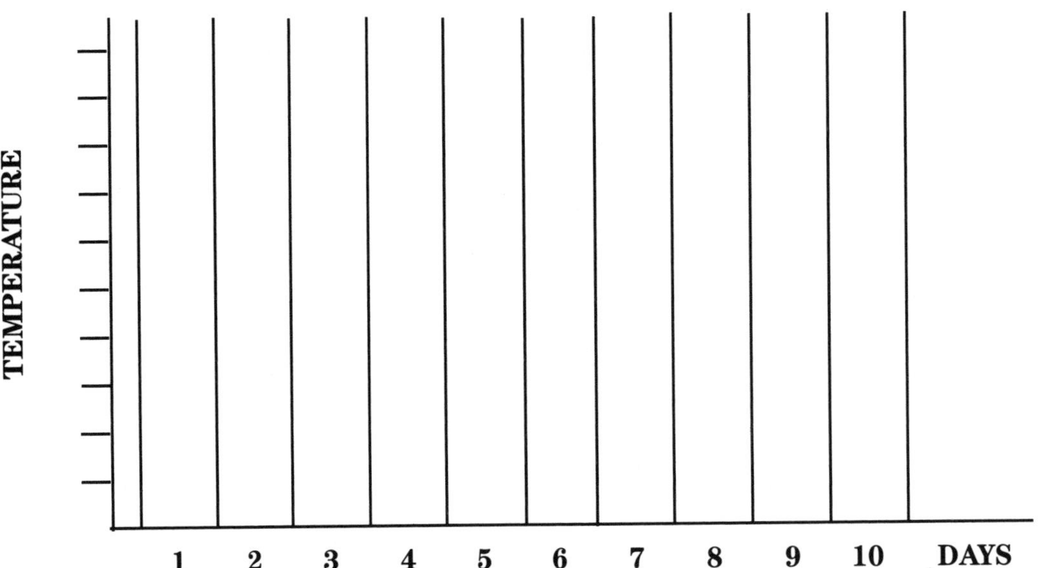

Answer these questions about your graph.

1. How many days were warmer then DAY 5?________________
2. What day was the warmest?__________Coldest?________
3. What was the difference between the warmest and coldest days?________________
4. Which days were colder then DAY 10?________________

Name_______________________________

AIR RESISTANCE

When you ride a bike you can feel the air against your face. You are feeling air resistance. The gasses in the air rub against anything trying to move through it. Cars and airplanes are made with smooth designs to decrease wind resistance or the resistance of the air. Parachutes are stretched out to catch the air. The air resistance slows the parachute to a safe speed.

When you watch a snowflake flutter to the ground, you may notice it falls much more slowly than a raindrop. The snowflake has more surface area. The resistance of the air has more surface to rub against, so it slows down the snowflake.

If you follow the directions below, you will see air resistance at work.

Make a helicopter.

1. Cut on the bold lines.

2. Fold on the dotted lines.

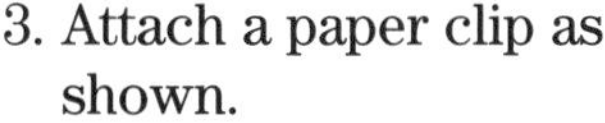

3. Attach a paper clip as shown.
4. Launch from a high place or toss into the air.

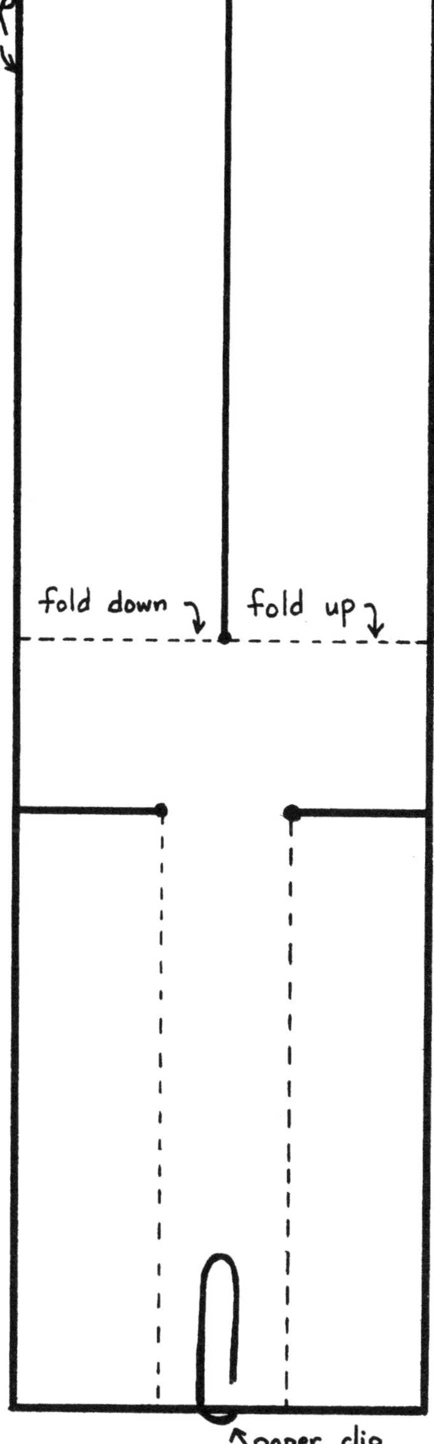

Name ______________________________

AN "AIRY" PUZZLE

Use the clues and words in the word box to help you solve the puzzle.

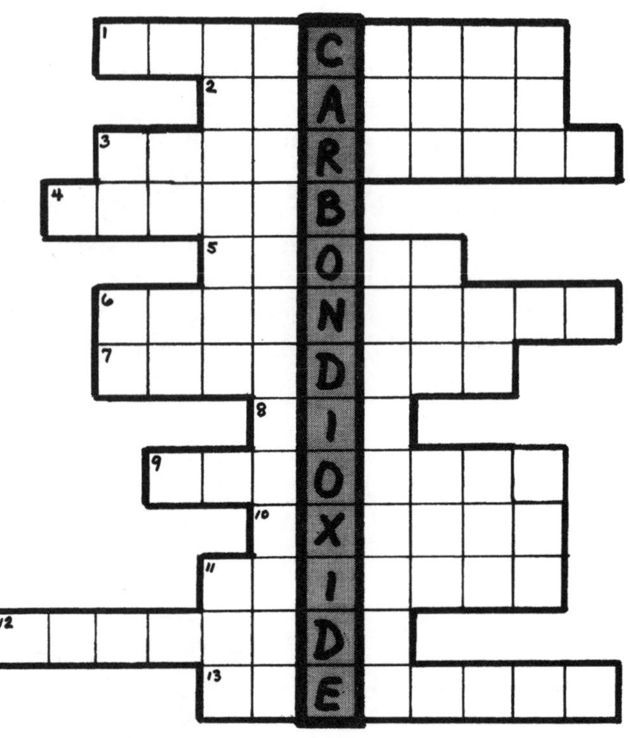

oxygen
humidity
aerosols
resistance
pressure
air
thermometer
altitude
absorb
molecules
climate
weather
ozone
greenhouse
atmosphere

CLUES:

1. Air ________ bounce around and bump into each other.
2. Meteorologists predict the _________ every day.
3. _________ is water that has evaporated into the air. (two words)
4. Warm air can _______ more water vapor than cool air.
5. The _________ layer protects the earth from harmful rays.
6. The __________ effect explains how the atmosphere traps heat.
7. The measure of ________ is the amount of water vapor in the air.
8. The mixture of gasses in the atmosphere is _________.
9. Salts, pollen, and dust are all _________.
10. __________ is about 21% of the air.
11. The average weather of an area over time is ________.
12. Sea level is the starting point of _________.
13. Air _______ is about 15 pounds per square inch at sea level.

Name ______________________________

AIR QUICK CHECK

Use the word box to help you complete the sentences.

evaporation	atmosphere	barometer	oxygen	nitrogen
troposphere	humidity	heat	aerosols	water vapor

1. The blanket of air surrounding the earth is our ____________________.

2. The layer of atmosphere where we live is called the ____________________.

3. Meteorologists use a ____________________ to measure the atmospheric pressure.

4. Most of the air, 78%, is ____ gas.

5. ____________________ is the amount of water vapor held in the air.

6. Tiny bits of salt, pollen, and dust in the air are ____________________.

7. The greenhouse effect is how the atmosphere traps ____________________.

Write "YES" for true and "NO" for not true.

8. ________Warm air is lighter and has less air pressure than cool air.
9. ________ Air pressure is nearly the same everywhere in the atmosphere.
10. ________ Convection is the circulation of air and heat around the atmosphere.
11. ________ People's activities may be changing the earth's climate.
12. ________ Air resistance acts to slow down anything moving through the air.
13. ________ Oceans heat more slowly and hold heat longer than land areas.
14. ________ Air pressure is about 15 pounds per square inch at sea level.

★ Think about the most interesting or important thing you have learned about air and the atmosphere. Write about it on the back of this sheet.

I'm going outside for some fresh air.

Environment Notes

Section Three

ECOLOGY

How Do We Fit In?

Name ______________________________

A PLANT WORD SEARCH

Circle each of these words you find in the word search. The words can be found down or across.

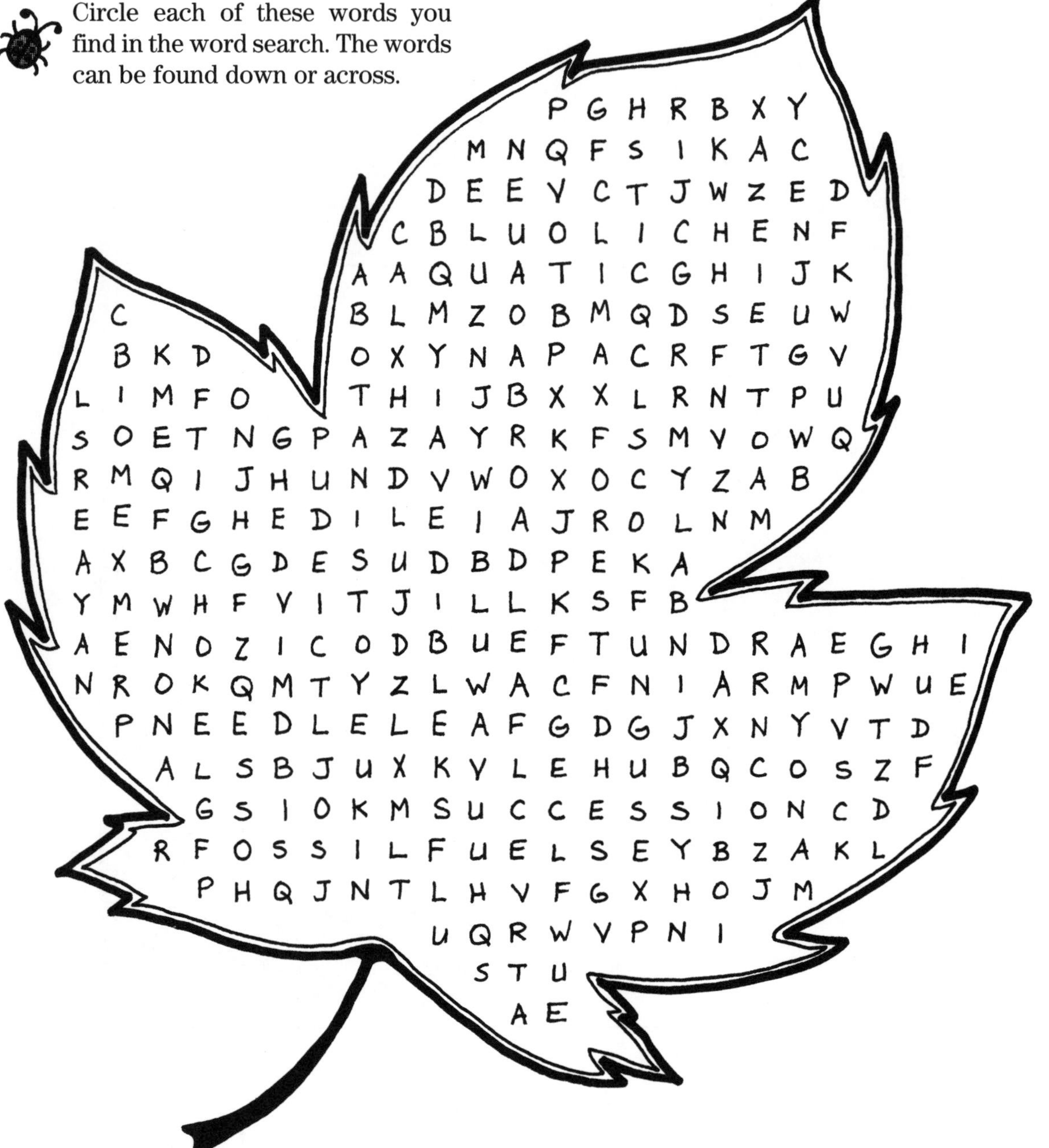

FOSSIL FUELS	CLIMAX FOREST	NEEDLELEAF	BROADLEAF
BIOME	BOTANIST	SUCCESSION	AQUATIC
LICHEN	EDIBLE	FUNGUS	TUNDRA

Name________________________________

PLANT HANDWRITING

roots ________________________________

____

leaves ________________________________

____

stem ________________________________

____

seed ________________________________

____

stamen ________________________________

____

pistal ________________________________

____

petal ________________________________

____

flower ________________________________

____

chlorophyll ________________________________

____

photosynthesis ________________________________

____

Name ______________________________

THE GREEN PROVIDERS

As you read this story, circle the correct word in each numbered box at the bottom of this sheet.

Your providers give you the things you need to live. You need food, clothing, and shelter as well as fresh air and water. All these 1.__________ and more are provided by the "green providers"—PLANTS! Plant's don't move 2.__________ like animals, but they can do one thing no animal has ever done. Plants make their own food. Chlorophyll gives plants their green 3._________. Chlorophyll also changes sunlight, water, and carbon dioxide into sugar 4.________ oxygen. This process is called photosynthesis.

All the food you eat comes 5._________ plants—all of it! Fruits and vegetables are easy to recognize as 6.________ foods. Bread and cereal are made with ground seeds from plants. You may 7.________ that meat, milk, and eggs certainly don't grow on plants. Actually they do. Every animal food that we 8.________ is grown by feeding the animals plant foods.

Do you ever wear jeans or t-shirts? If so, you are wearing plants. Cotton fiber is one of the most common 9.________ in clothing. The home you live in is probably made with many wood products. Lumber is important for all types of construction including homes, businesses, and furniture. Your home may be heated by a wood-burning stove. Even fossil fuels such as coal and oil come from ancient plants.

Because 10.__________ are rooted to one place, they help to hold the soil. Plants absorb fresh water and release it slowly into the atmosphere. They clean the air and give off oxygen. Many medicines come from plants. The paper this is written on came from plant fibers. Plants are truly green providers.

"Photosynthesis" means "to build with light."

1.	2.	3.	4.	5.
animals things providers	by around after	smell color sound	and but beside	from over around
6.	**7.**	**8.**	**9.**	**10.**
plant animal sugar	use change think	play drink eat	materials foods fruits	plants animals people

Name________________________________

PLANT SURVIVAL

As you read this story, circle the correct word in each numbered box at the bottom of this sheet.

Plants have been around for millions of years—some for more than 3,000 million years! How have they survived so long? Plants have adapted to nearly every environment on 1.________. They live on high mountain slopes and in the arid deserts. 2.___________ flourish on the high seas and even in underground caves. To survive, plants have evolved many "tricks" to protect 3.__________ and to get some animals to work for them.

Plants stay in one place. They cannot run away from enemies as animals can. All animal life depends on 4.__________ for food. How do plants defend themselves against becoming a picnic for any animal who happens by? Also, since the plants cannot move around, how can they spread their seeds from place to place?

Plants are not as defenseless as 5._________ may seem. Thistles have thorns and 6.________ to keep predators away. Poison ivy produces chemicals that sting. Milkweed oozes a sticky glue called latex for protection from chewing insects. We actually 7.____________ a surprisingly small number of wild plants because they are unpleasant and dangerous. Scientists are very interested in plant defenses. Many medicines have been 8.__________ from plant chemicals.

Plants sometimes use tricks to attract insects, birds, and animals. Plants use attractive colors and sweet 9._________ to attract insects to their flowers. Insects carry pollen from flower to 10.____________ so new seeds will grow. Birds eat juicy fruits, like cherries, and carry the pits far from the parent tree. In this way plants can move to new locations where they may thrive.

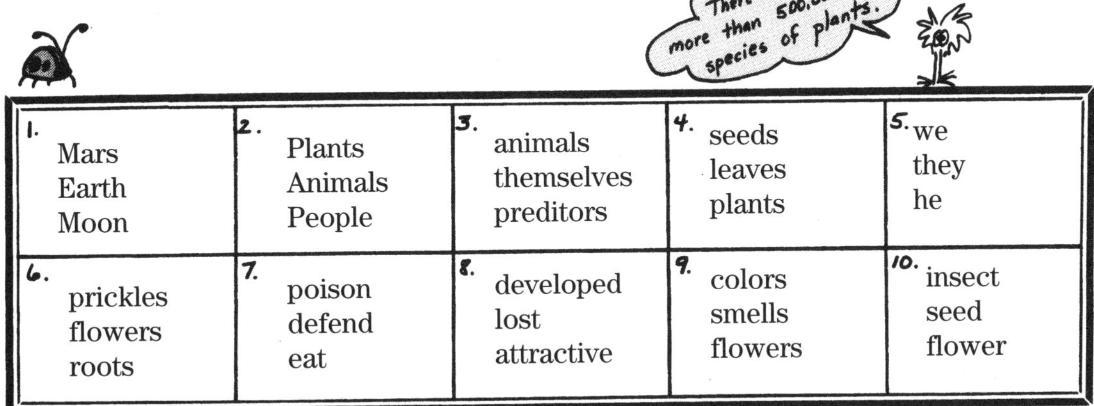

1.	2.	3.	4.	5.
Mars Earth Moon	Plants Animals People	animals themselves preditors	seeds leaves plants	we they he
6. prickles flowers roots	**7.** poison defend eat	**8.** developed lost attractive	**9.** colors smells flowers	**10.** insect seed flower

Name ______________________________

PORTRAIT OF A PLANT

You are going to find out more about all plants by researching one special plant. An encyclopedia will help you choose a plant to study. You may choose something common such as a dandelion or an exotic plant like the strangler fig. Try to select a plant that no one else is studying.

Locate one of the following articles in an encyclopedia: "Plants," "Vegetables," or "Trees." Following each article should be a list of related articles. These lists will include the names of many plants, shrubs, and trees. Use these lists to help you choose a plant of your own.

Answer the questions below about your special plant. Try to use complete sentences and include as many interesting details as possible.

In the magnifying glass draw your plant's leaf or flower.

1. What is the common name of your plant?

____

2. What is the scientific name of your plant?

____

3. To what plant family does your plant belong? ______________________________

____

4. What does your plant look like? ______________________________

____

____

5. In which biome is your plant found? Describe the climate there. ____________

____

____

Name__________________________________

PORTRAIT OF A PLANT, CONTINUED

6. Describe your plant's community including its plant and animal neighbors. ____________

7. How does your plant reproduce? ____________

8. How does your plant defend itself? ____________

9. What do you think everyone should know about your special plant? ____________

10. What is the most important thing you learned about your special plant? ____________

On another paper draw a picture of your plant. Try to show its unique features.

Name ______________________________

I worked with ______________________

____

PLANT SCAVENGER HUNT

Plants provide us with many things we use every day. Today you will search for some of these things. You will work with at least two other people. Your team should work together so that each person finds and records each item. In most scavenger hunts the searchers collect items. You will collect descriptions.

Your teacher will tell you the boundaries of the hunt. You may also have a time limit. As you search, be considerate of the other people in and around your classroom and school. Walk quietly and use quiet voices. Have discussions where you won't disturb others.

As you locate each item, write a description of your finding. Include as much detail as possible. Tell where it was found and how it is used.

Try to find unusual items. You will get extra points if your group is the only one to list a particular item.

The first item is done for you to help you get started. Good luck!

---

edible seed *Barbara has sunflower seeds in her lunch box. She is going to eat the seeds and spit the shells.*

cardboard ______________________________

____

plant larger than you ______________________________

____

lumber ______________________________

____

plant stem we eat ______________________________

____

cotton garment ______________________________

____

Name________________________________

paper ____

____

wooden furniture ____

____

edible flower ____

____

handy wooden object ____________________________________

____

paper without printing __________________________________

____

wood used for fun ______________________________________

____

seed ____

____

plant product above your head ____________________________

____

fuel from plants ______________________________________

____

plant product you can touch ______________________________

____

grass or lawn ____

____

When you have finished, give yourself 1 point for each item you found. Compare your findings with other groups. Give yourself 1 bonus point for each unique item. Add the 5 special bonus points if you earned them. Write your total in the star.

Name ________________________________

PLANT SUCCESSION

Ready:

violently spared community succession alga fungus Photosynthesis spores rhyzoids seedlings

1. A word that rhymes with "doors" is ______________________.

2. ______________________ means "to put together with light."

3. A ______________________ is a plant that cannot make its own food.

4. Something that happens quickly and with great force happens ______________________.

5. The word ______________________ has a silent "h."

In Washington State, in May of 1980, Mount St. Helens violently erupted. The power of the mountain's blast leveled hundreds of square miles. Neither plants nor animals were spared. Today, Mount St. Helens is green. The plant community is recovering. It will take many, many years, but the forest will return to the mountain. The process of its renewal is called plant succession.

Each kind of plant needs just the right amount of sunshine and shade. The plants growing in one area change as new plants grow and shade out the old plants. In this way, one kind of plant prepares the way for another.

Lichen is a plant that can grow without soil, even on rock! Lichen is actually two plants living together—alga and fungus. The fungus absorbs and holds water for the alga to use in photosynthesis. The alga makes enough food for both plants. Lichen produces carbonic acid which helps disintegrate rock and form pockets of soil.

Name___________________________________

PLANT SUCCESSION, CONTINUED

Moss spores are blown into soil pockets by the wind. Mosses have root-like rhyzoids to anchor the plant and absorb water. Moss squeezes out lichen because it is better suited to the particular environment. Decaying lichen and moss help form more soil. Grasses and other thin-leaved plants love the sun. They grow quickly in the shadeless areas. The grasses have long roots and grow taller than the mosses. The moss is shaded out.

Seedlings of bushes like blackberry and thimbleberry grow more slowly than the grasses. Tree seedlings grow in the protective shade of the bushes. As these trees grow out from under the canopy of the bushes, the maturing trees shade the bushes. The bushes die out for lack of sun. Later, shade-loving plants such as ferns and salal will move in under the trees in the deep shade. The trees are the last link in the chain of plant succession.

Plant succession is complete when the land is covered by a climax forest. The climax forest is made up of trees and plants best suited to the soil and climate. In North America the eastern hardwoods are the climax forest east of the Mississippi River and north into parts of southern Canada. The western and northern regions of North America have poorer soil and more severe weather. Here the needleleaf conifers make up the climax forest. In some climates and soil conditions the climax of plant succession may be grasses. Such an area is the prairie regions of central North America.

1. Plant succession happens very (quickly, slowly).

2. Each kind of plant needs just the right amount of ____________________ and ____________________.

3. Two plants, alga and fungus, live together to form ____________________.

4. Plants that grow more slowly, but taller, shade out lower-growing plants. (YES, NO)

5. The last stage of plant succession is the (natural, old-growth, climax) forest.

6. What type of plant has root-like rhyzoids?____________________

7. ____________________ are sun-loving plants.

8. ____________________ grow in areas of deep shade under the trees of the climax forest.

Name ___________________________

SPECIAL PARTS, SPECIAL JOBS

Plants have four main parts. Each part of the plant has a special job to do. A plant's roots have several jobs. They absorb water and minerals from the soil. Roots also store food for the plant. They anchor the plant securely in the soil and keep it upright.

The leaves of a plant contain chlorophyll. This is where food is made by the process of photosynthesis. The leaves also have special pores to take in carbon dioxide.

A plant's stem is like a bundle of tubes. These tubes carry water and dissolved minerals from the roots to the leaves. The stem also moves food to all parts of the plant. Of course, the stem has the job of holding up the plant's leaves and flowers.

The flower is the plant's reproductive part. The flower becomes fruit and contains the plant's seeds. The flower of a plant has four main parts. Although flowers come in many shapes and forms, all four parts are present in any flower. Each part of the flower has a special job to do.

The flower's sepals are usually green. The sepals are tough and protect the bud and maturing flower. The sepals are usually found at the base of the mature flower.

Flower petals are usually delicate structures. They are most often a color other than green. This makes them more easily seen in contrast to the green of the plant. Petal color and sweet scent attract insects to the flower. Insects help the plant reproduce by spreading pollen from one flower to another.

Pollen grains cover the pollen sacs at the ends of the flower's stamens. The stamen usually looks like a thin tube with the dusty-looking pollen sac on the end.

The pistal of the flower is usually in the center. The pistal contains the cells that will become seeds. The end of the pistal is moist or sticky to catch and hold pollen. A tube will carry the pollen down the pistal to the seeds.

Name________________________________

SPECIAL PARTS, SPECIAL JOBS, CONTINUED

Use the underlined words from the article to help you label the plant and flower parts on the picture below.

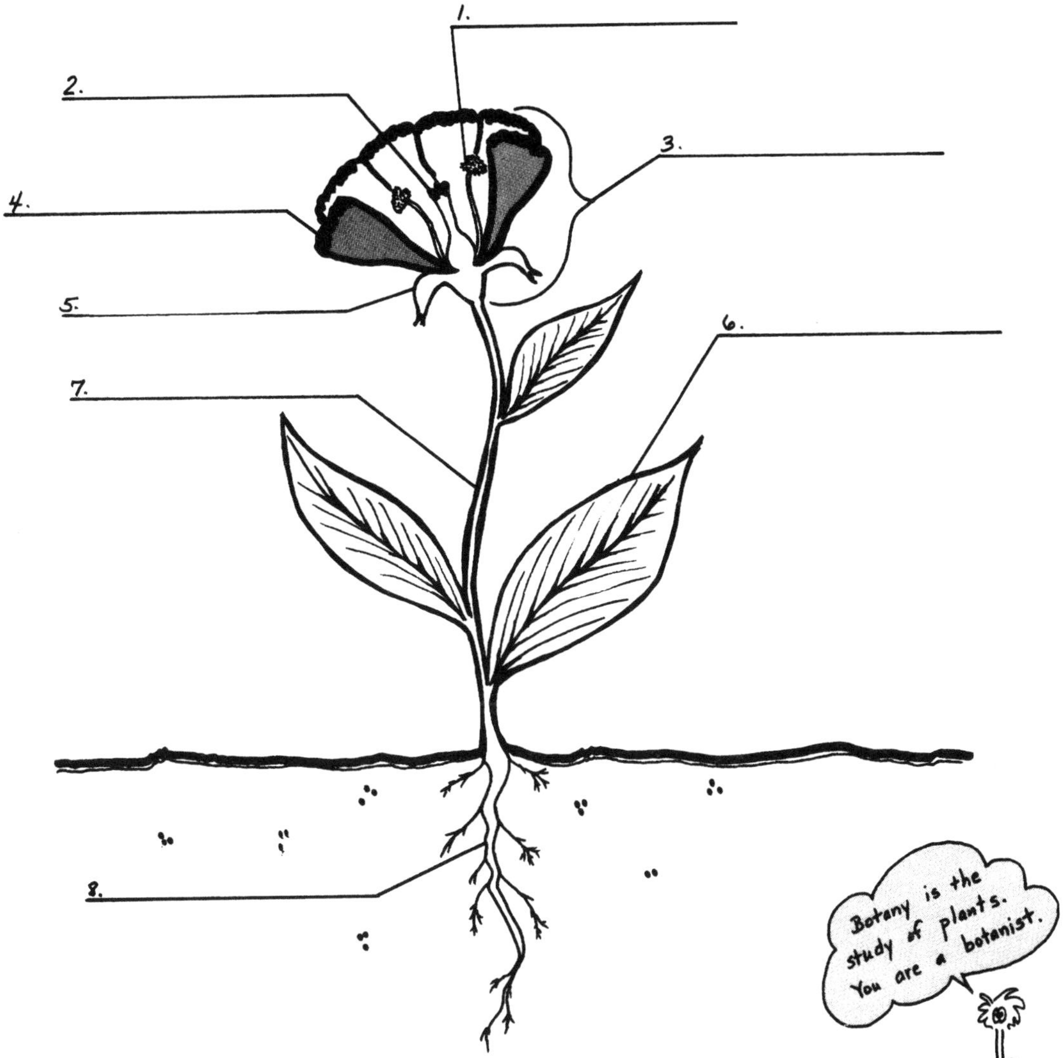

1. ________________
2. ________________
3. ________________
4. ________________
5. ________________
6. ________________
7. ________________
8. ________________

Where is most of the plant's chlorophyll found and what does it do?

____

____

____

Name ______________________

BIOME RIDDLES

You are a member of your school community. Your family and neighborhood are communities. Plants live in communities, too. Plant communities are called biomes.

Plants grow where conditions are just right. Different plants have different needs for water, sunlight, soil, and temperature. Each biome has different conditions and, therefore, different plants. Botanists divide the earth into five plant biomes.

The tundra biome is cold and treeless. Arctic regions near the North Pole in Europe, Asia, and North America are tundra regions. The tundra is frozen several feet down. Only the top 12 inches of soil thaw in the summer. The tundra is dry, getting only 6-10 inches of rain each year. Plants of the tundra grow in low clumps out of the bitter wind. Mosses, lichen, and wildflowers grow on the tundra.

About one-fifth of the earth's land is desert. A huge desert area covers much of northern Africa. Temperatures here can rise above 100 degrees F. Part of the year can also be very cold. Because there is very little moisture in the desert, plants are spread out. This gives each plant room to spread out roots over a wide area to collect water. Some plants, like the succulents, store water in their thick stems and leaves. Cacti store water. Palms, yuccas, and wildflowers live in the desert biome.

Grasslands are regions with conditions too poor to support many trees. Grasses are the main varieties of plants. The Great Plains of North America are grasslands. Most natural grasslands are now used for farming. Wheat, oats, barley, and corn grow well here. This is no surprise—all of these crops are grasses!

Forest covers about one-third of the earth's land area. Three different types of forests are included in this biome. They are needleleaf forests, broadleaf forests, and tropical rain forests. All forest regions have dense stands of trees. Every continent except Antarctica have forest biome areas.

Aquatic regions include both fresh and salt water. Most plants grow in shallows and near the surface of the water because they need sunlight. Algae are very important water plants. It is part of plankton and a rich source of food for aquatic animals. Cattails, bulrushes, kelp, and eelgrass are all plants of the aquatic region's biome.

Name________________________________

BIOME RIDDLES, CONTINUED

Solve each riddle by writing the name of the correct biome on the line following the riddle. Look back at the article if you need help.

1. I see large trees. This biome covers one-third of the earth's land area. I could be on any continent except Antarctica. Where am I?

____

2. It is cold and dry here. I see low-growing clumps of moss and wildflowers. I am near the North Pole. The ground stays frozen most of the year. Where am I?

____

3. I am standing beside a tall cactus. It is hot and dry here. The plants grow far apart to draw in as much water as possible. Where am I?

____

4. There are many farms here. I see corn, wheat, and barley growing. Grasses cover the gently rolling hills as far as I can see. Where am I?

____

Write your own riddle for the aquatic regions biome. ____________________

____

____

____

In which biome is your home?

____

Name ______________________________

TROPICAL TREASURE

tropical
biome
equator
combined
lush
mahogany
teak
exported
calculate
temporarily

1. A word that rhymes with "brush" is ________________.
2. The opposite of "imported" is ____________________.
3. ______________ and ______________ are types of trees that live in the rain forest.
4. Areas near the equator are called ________________.
5. Something that is only used for a short time is used ____________________.
6. A word that means "taken all together" is ______________.

The tropical rain forest is part of the earth's forest biome. The rain forest is hot and humid. Temperatures here usually stay between 68 and 93 degrees F. At least 80 inches of rain fall each year. In some areas more than 160 inches of rain fall each year. That's more than 13 feet of rain! No wonder it is called the rain forest.

Tropical rain forests cover parts of Central America, Africa, and Asia. The largest is the Amazon rain forest of South America. It covers nearly one-third of the entire continent. Because they are near the equator, the rain forests have 12 hours of sunlight every day. Each day here is much the same as another. There are no seasons in the rain forest. It is the perfect environment for plants to grow. More species of plants and animals live in the tropical rain forest than in all the rest of the world combined. Rain forests cover less than 10% of the earth's surface, but are home to more than 50% of the earth's plant and animal species. Scientists believe that there are millions of species that have not even been discovered yet!

Name ___________________________________

TROPICAL TREASURE, CONTINUED

The tropical rain forests are important to all of us. The lush plant life produces the oxygen that all animal life needs. The rain forest absorbs and releases huge amounts of water. Without the rain forest, weather around the world would be very different. Some products from the rain forest are used all over the world. Vanilla, coffee, tea, cinnamon, nutmeg, chocolate, and bananas are some of the many rain forest products. Mahogany and teak are types of lumber exported from rain forest countries.

Rain forest areas are shrinking at an alarming rate. The forest is being cut down for timber and cleared for farming. The clearing method is called "slash and burn." The large trees are cut down and burned. The ashes temporarily enrich the poor soil. After a few years the land won't grow crops anymore and is abandoned. Another section of the rain forest is cleared to replace the worn-out land. The poor soil becomes barren waste.

Scientists calculate that up to one-half of all the rain forest has already been destroyed. Many people are trying to save the remaining rain forest. The governments of rain forest countries are working with worldwide organizations. They are trying to teach people about the importance of the rain forests and why they need to be preserved.

1. The rain forest is (cool, warm, hot) and humid.
2. How much sunlight does the rain forest receive each day? ______________________
3. What are three products of the rain forest? ______________________, ______________________, and ______________________.
4. The clearing method used in the rain forest is called ______________ and ______________.
5. Scientists believe that there are ______________ of plant and animal species waiting to be discovered.
6. The rain forest is home to more than (16%, 50%, 70%) of the earth's plants and animals.
7. The rain forest produces a large amount of valuable carbon dioxide. (YES, NO)

Name ______________________________

SCRAMBLED TREES

Unscramble the letters to make the names of seven familiar trees. Draw a line connecting the name of each tree to the picture of its leaf. The first one is done for you.

lwiolw *willow* ____________ •

ncettush ____________ •

neip ____________ •

draec ____________ •

lemkohc ____________ •

pleam ____________ •

dnotoctwoo ____________ •

★ Which of these trees is broadleaf? *willow,* ____________

★ ____________________________

Which are needleleaf? ____________________

____

Name_________________________________

TRANSPIRATION

Plants draw water up their stems to their leaves and flowers. Much of the water evaporates through small openings in the leaves called stomata. This process is called transpiration.

You can see transpiration in a simple experiment. You will need a white flower, a glass of water, and some food coloring. Use the food coloring to dye the water. The more color you use, the more color your flower will show. Make a fresh cut at the bottom of the flower's stem with a sharp knife. Put the flower stem into the glass. Place the glass in a sunny window. Check the flower every 15 minutes. You should be able to see the color in the flower in about one hour.

You may like to try playing with this experiment. What might happen if you split the bottom of the stem and put the two parts in different colors of water? What if you put a flower in red coloring for one hour and in blue for another hour? What else might you try?

Number these steps in the correct order to complete the experiment described above.

___1___ Gather together: white flower, glass of water, and food dye.

_______ Make a fresh cut at the bottom of the stem.

_______ Put the flower stem in the glass.

_______ Place the glass in a sunny window.

_______ Use food dye to color the water in the glass.

_______ Look at the flower about every 15 minutes.

Plants move water up their stems to their leaves and flowers. What is this process called?

★ ________________________________ ★

Name ______________________________

HOW TALL?

How can you measure the height of a tree without climbing it or cutting it down? If you can multiply, you can make a very good estimate of how tall the tree is.

Have a friend stand beside the tree. You need to stand back where you can see the top of the tree easily. Holding a stick at arm's length, line up the top of the stick with the top of your friend's head. Make a mark on the stick where you see the bottom of your friend's feet. Next, line up the top of the stick with the treetop. Mark the stick where you see the bottom of the tree. Now you can work out the height of the tree.

The two marks on the stick show your friend's height and the tree's height. If your friend is 5 feet tall and the tree is 8 times as tall as your friend, the tree is 40 feet tall!

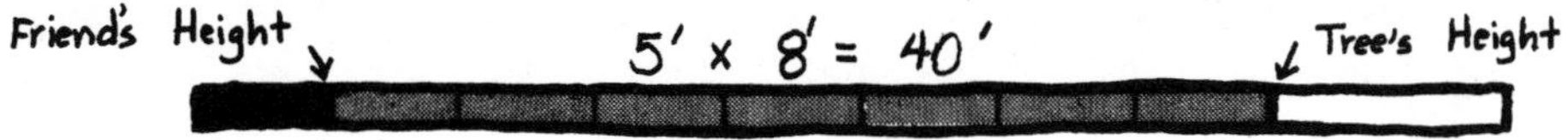

Work out the height of each tree if your friend is 5 feet tall and the tree measurement is:

WORK SPACE

1. 6 times as tall ________ feet
2. 9 times as tall ________
3. 16 times as tall ________
4. 20 times as tall ________
5. 7 times as tall ________
6. 58 times as tall ________
7. 13 times as tall ________
8. 4 times as tall ________

You can measure tall buildings this way, too.

Name________________________________

PLANT QUICK CHECK

Use the word box to help you complete the sentences.

1. The green color in plants that helps them produce food is ______________________.

Lichen	chlorophyll	transpiration	flower	succession
Photosynthesis	roots	mosses	precipitation	biomes

2. The world's plant communities are called ______________________.

3. ______________________ is how plants draw water up into their leaves.

4. In plant ______________________one type of plant is shaded out by another.

5. ______________________ is actually two plants—alga and fungus.

6. ______________________ is the process by which plants make food from water and sunlight.

7. The ______________________ is the reproductive part of the plant.

8. __________ All food you eat actually comes from plants

Write "YES" for true and "NO" for not true.

9. __________ Plants are really defenseless against insects and other pests.

10. __________ Food is the only wide-spread, human use of plants.

11. __________ Rain forest soil is very rich in nutrients and minerals.

12. __________ Each part of a plant has a special job to do for the plant.

13. __________ Pollen drops to the ground and starts a new plant.

14. __________ The climax forest is the last level of plant succession.

Think about the most interesting or important thing you have learned about plants. Write about it on the back of this sheet.

Name ______________________________

AN ANIMAL WORD SEARCH

Circle each of the words you find in the word search. The words can be found either down or across.

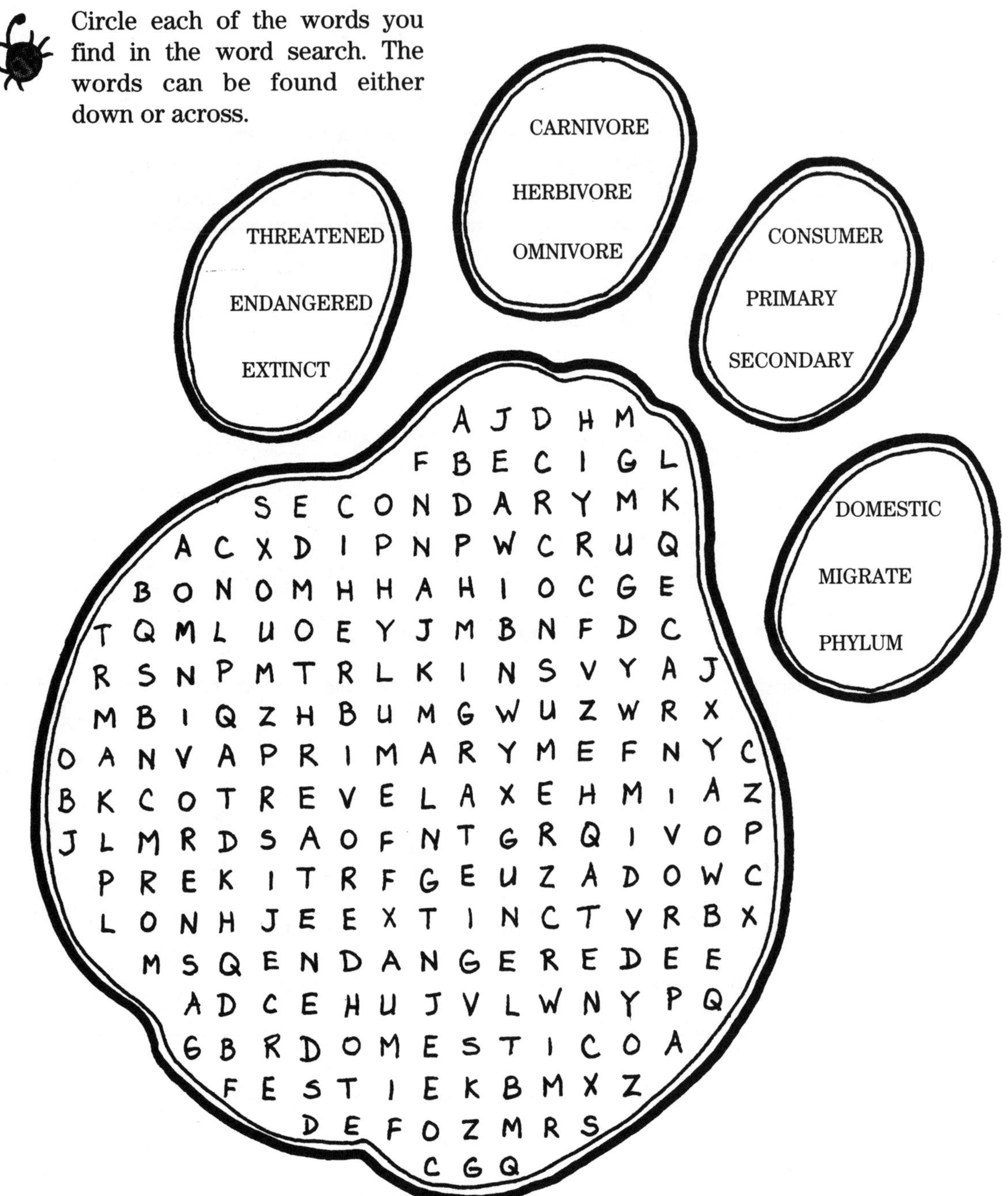

Name________________________________

ANIMAL HANDWRITING

decomposers________________________________

____

adaptation________________________________

____

species________________________________

____

camouflage________________________________

____

habitat________________________________

____

niche________________________________

____

ecosystem________________________________

____

food chain________________________________

____

balance of nature________________________________

____

survival________________________________

Name ______________________________

ANIMALS, ANIMALS, ANIMALS

Scientists who study animals are called zoologists.

As you read this story, circle the correct word in each numbered box at the bottom of this sheet.

The bodies and habits of animals have adapted to climates and conditions around the world. Penguins are 1.________ suited to their aquatic, polar homes. They would find life very difficult in the canopy of the Amazon rain forest. A jellyfish wouldn't last 2.__________ in the desert of the southwestern United States. Adaptation has taken thousands of years. During that time animals have developed many ways of fitting in to their different environments.

Each animal species is unique. Each is suited to its special 3.__________. However, all animal species are similar in some important ways. Animals cannot make their own food as 4.__________ do. They must eat. Some animals 5.__________ plants. Some animal preditors eat the meat of other animals. Some animals eat most anything—meat or vegetable!

6.__________ can do something that plants cannot do. Animals move under their own power. The ability to 7.________ makes animals able to find food and avoid enemies. These are very handy skills for survival.

All animals need oxygen. Oxygen helps 8.________ make energy from the food they eat. Some animals, like you, 9.________ air with their lungs. Some animals have gills and take oxygen from water. Others simply absorb the oxygen they need through their skin.

Animals are everywhere. They live all over the 10.__________. Animals crawl, walk, and run on land. They swim and float in lakes, rivers, and seas. Animals soar on the currents of air high in the sky. Scientists know about a million species of animals. There are probably millions more waiting to be discovered.

1.	2.	3.	4.	5.
well ill poorly	long short even	unique plant environment	animals people plants	grow make eat
6.	**7.**	**8.**	**9.**	**10.**
Plants People Animals	eat move make	plants animals species	breathe eat grow	moon sun earth

Name___________________________________

CLASSIFYING ANIMALS

As you read this story, circle the correct word in each numbered box at the bottom of this page.

The animal kingdom is a diverse group. Its members are 1.___________ and varied. Some animals are so small that you need a microscope to see them. Others weigh several tons. The oyster, camel, amoeba, gorilla, and whale are all part of the 2.____________ kingdom.

There are many ways to classify animals. Usually they are 3.____________ by common characteristics. Animals can be grouped by where they live. Whether they are wild or tame is a way to 4.____________ animals. Sometimes animals are grouped by whether they are warm-blooded or cold-blooded. Even the number of legs can separate animals into 5.____________.

Zoologists have a special system for classifying animals. They group 6.____________ with similar body features and habits. A phylum is a large grouping of animals. All animals that have backbones 7.____________ to the phylum, vertabrata. This phylum includes fish, reptiles, amphibians, birds, and mammals.

Animals are further grouped into classes, orders, families, 8.___________ species. Your family's pet dog belongs to the class, Mammalia, and to the order, Carnivora. Its family is Canidae. Your 9.____________ even has its own scientific name—Canis Familiaris!

Every animal known to scientists fits into this 10.____________ of classification. Jellyfish, earthworm, slugs, spiders, and turtles have their places. Sharks, frogs, kangaroos, elephants, and dolphins have their places, too. Even you have a spot in the scientific classification of animals.

1.	2.	3.	4.	5.
few small many	plant kingdom animal	grouped lost similarly	classify share save	groups piles herd
6.	**7.**	**8.**	**9.**	**10.**
plants animals people	classify belong share	and nor but	dog family group	group animal system

Name ______________________________

BATTLE FOR SURVIVAL

Ready:

survival adaptability scarce habitat exhausted migrate hibernate camouflage protection surroundings

1. ________________ is a one-syllable word.
2. Something that is "worn out" or used up is ________________.
3. ________________ is a six-syllable word.
4. Animals that sleep through times of harsh conditions are said to ________________.
5. It is hard to see an animal that has very good ________________.
6. ________________ means about the same as "environment."

Set:

Animals are in a constant struggle to keep their species alive. To win the battle for survival, animals need food, water, and a place to raise their young. The animals alive today have adapted their environment and won the battle. Many species have died out. They could not adapt or find their basic needs.

Every environment on the earth is home to animals. Over millions of years animals have adapted to very different environments from the ocean depths to mountain tops. Adaptability is the key to an animal's survival. For a species to continue, its members must live long enough to raise young. Animals who adapt to changes have a better chance of staying alive. Animals must find food even when food is scarce. They need to move when habitat is lost or exhausted. They also need to defend themselves and their young against enemies.

Many special behaviors help animals to survive. Bears and bats hibernate during severe weather. Snow geese, Monarch butterflies, and caribou migrate to avoid harsh winter conditions. Many animals cover large areas each day in search of food and water.

Name_______________________________

BATTLE FOR SURVIVAL, CONTINUED

Animals defend themselves against enemies in several ways. Some creatures hide. Many seek thick cover of forest plants. Some use camouflage and hide by blending with their environment. Indian leaf butterflies have wings that look just like a dead leaf. Chameleons can even change color to match their surroundings. Opossum go limp when an enemy is near. Its enemy will think the opossum is already dead and leave it alone. Clams and turtles have hard shells to protect them from being eaten. Porcupine have sharp quills to fend off predators. Antelope and deer have long legs and can usually outrun their enemies.

Some animals find protection in large groups. Many fish school together for safety. Birds often form flocks for the same reason. Many large animals of the grasslands, such as zebra, live in herds. Some animals even form groups with different species to help both survive. Tickbirds perch on the back of rhinos where they can eat the insects from the backs of the rhinos. In return, the birds warn their hosts of approaching danger.

Many insects taste bad or are poisonous. Certainly, you can think of many animals who use strong teeth and sharp claws for defense.

1. Where do animals live on the earth?__________________

2. What three things do all animal species need to win the battle for survival?

   __________________, __________________, and __________________

3. Animals who adapt to changes have a better chance of staying alive. (YES, NO)

4. Bats and bears (migrate, adapt, hibernate) during severe weather.

5. How do chameleons defend against their enemies? ______________________

6. Fish, birds, and large grassland animals live in large groups for __________________.

7. To win the battle for survival, animals must __________________ to changes in their environment.

Name ______________________________

THE BALANCE OF NATURE

Every plant and animal in an ecosystem is important. Each organism has a role to play in the success of the ecosystem. The role of a plant or animal plays is its ecological niche.

Animals and plants depend on one another. Without plants there would be no oxygen for animals to breathe. Without insects many plants could not produce seeds. Predators keep many species from over-population. Without decomposers there would be no rich soil.

In an ecosystem the number of one kind of animal is called a population. The size of animal populations stays about the same most of the time. This is nature in balance. If something happens to change one population, the balance of nature is upset. The whole ecosystem is affected.

If the weather is particularly good one year there may be more plants than usual. Mice and rabbits who eat the plants are well-fed and healthy. They have more babies and more survive. Because there are plenty of mice and rabbits to eat, more foxes than usual survive. All of the mice and rabbits eat so many plants that there is not enough to go around. Many of the mice and rabbits starve. There is less food available for foxes and some weaken and die. Nature returns to its normal balance.

Plants, mice, rabbits, and foxes are part of a simple food chain. Usually bigger animals eat smaller ones, but not always. Plants are the earth's only providers. Plants can use the sun's energy to make food. This process is called photosynthesis. Animals who eat plants are called primary consumers. Mice, cows, and deer are primary consumers. Foxes, lions, and seals are all secondary consumers. Food chains are much like pyramids. It takes many plants to feed one rabbit and it takes many rabbits to feed one fox.

Most ecosystems have complicated systems of producers and consumers. These overlapping food chains are called food webs. Where do people fit in the food chain?

Use this article to help you complete the next page.

Name_______________________________

THE BALANCE OF NATURE, CONTINUED

In each level of the food chain, draw pictures or write in the names of animal or plants that fit in each one.

Secondary Consumers:
Primary Consumers:
Producers:

In an area of North America an ecosystem was in balance. About 4,000 deer ranged a large area of scrub forest. Wolves kept the deer population stable. Because the wolves occasionally killed sheep, ranchers trapped and shot most of the wolves. Tell what you think will happen. (If you need more space, use the back of this sheet.)

____

____

____

____

Name ______________________________

THE CLEAN-UP CREW

Ready:

carcass
scavenger
decomposer
predator
cycle
minerals
nutrients
compost
humus
ecosystem

1. The word from the list that has a "y" that makes the long "i" sound is__________________.
2. A __________________ kills and eats other animals.
3. A __________________ eats other animals' leftovers.
4. __________________ and __________________ are decaying matter that enrich the soil.
5. The body of a dead animal is a __________________.

The food chain doesn't stop with the predators. The earth's food chain is a cycle. That means that it goes all the way around like a circle. There is no end. What happens to the predators? When animals die, their bodies are broken down by nature's clean-up crew.

Each day tons of once-living material fall onto the ground. In a short time we would be buried under leaves, dead animal carcasses, fallen trees, and our own wastes if not for scavengers and decomposers.

The scavengers are not always the best-liked or most beautiful animals, but they do a very important job. Scavengers—like vultures, hyenas, and oppossum—rid the environment of preditors' leftovers. Sexton beetles actually bury small dead animals and birds.

Name________________________________

THE CLEAN-UP CREW, CONTINUED

All of the minerals and nutrients on the earth are used over and over. The building blocks of your lunch sandwich might once have been dinner for a stegosaurus or part of an oak tree that gave shade to a pioneer family. The way minerals and nutrients are broken down and returned to the earth is by decomposing.

Insects, worms, and bacteria do more than just get dead matter out of the way. They enrich the soil so that plants have the nutrients they need to grow. Decomposers, like the dung beetle, turn animal droppings into rich compost for fertile soil. Earthworms break down decaying matter called humus. They enrich the soil. These little decay experts even loosen and stir the soil. This aerated soil helps plants grow healthy roots.

In every ecosystem on earth from oceans to forests, scavengers and decomposers are cleaning the environment. They are freeing nutrients to return to the earth. These nutrients feed the plants. The cycle is complete and nature is in balance.

1. Scavengers don't really help the environment very much. (YES, NO)
2. All of the minerals and ______________________ on the earth are used over and over.
3. Insects, worms, and bacteria are all ______________________ .
4. The earth's food chain is a (line, cycle, hill) that goes around.
5. Vultures, hyenas, and jackals are all ______________________ .
6. ______________________ need the enriched soil made by the decomposers.

Name ______________________

THREATENED, ENDANGERED, EXTINCT

There are no dinosaurs alive today. There are no mastodons or saber-toothed cats. These animals are extinct. Extinct means that none of these animals are still alive. These animals died out of natural causes. They couldn't find enough food, the climate changed, or they were eaten by predators.

Some characteristics make some species more likely to become extinct. Animals that have few babies have a harder time surviving than other animals that have many babies. The same is true of animals whose babies take a long time to grow up. Animals that eat only one kind of food are in danger if that food is scarce.

Not long ago only natural causes made animal species die out. Now many species are in danger because of the way people behave. One of the most serious problems people make for animals is the destruction of their homes and habitats. More and more people need more and more food and other things. They build farms and cities where wild animals used to live. The animals have less and less natural habitat.

People also hunt and catch wild animals for many uses. Animals are killed for food, trophies, or simply for fun. Many animals are killed for their fur. Some are killed for their teeth or horns. Animals are trapped for pets, zoos, and private collectors. Many animals die for every live one taken from the wild. Wild animals also have to compete with domestic animals for food.

Many animal species are losing the battle for survival. Some—like the American black bear, the red kangaroo, and the desert tortoise—are threatened. Threatened means that if their populations get any smaller, these species will be in danger of becoming extinct. The Asian elephant, the humpback whale, and the orangutan are endangered. Endangered means that they are so rare that they need help if they are to survive.

Many people are working to save the endangered animals. In 1941 there were only 23 whooping cranes in the world. Zoologists began raising whopping crane chicks. The crane's habitat was protected. Today there are more than 200 whooping cranes. They are coming back from the very edge of extinction. Other species can be saved as well.

Use this article to help you complete the next page.

Name ____________________

THREATENED, ENDANGERED, EXTINCT, CONTINUED

 Tell what each of these words mean. Use as much detail as you can.

THREATENED: ____________________

____

____

____

ENDANGERED: ____________________

____

____

____

EXTINCT: ____________________

____

____

What are some of the reasons that animal species are becoming extinct? ____________________

____

____

____

____

Tell how people can help animals that are threatened or endangered. If you need more space, use the back of this sheet. ____________________

____

____

Name ______________________________

ENDANGERED INTERVIEW

Below is a list of endangered animals. Your teacher may give you more animals to add to the list. Put stars by three animals that you think you would like to know more about.

AMERICAN BLACK BEAR	AYE-AYE	CHEETAH
CHIMPANZEE	CALIFORNIA CONDOR	MUSK DEER
ASIAN ELEPHANT	PEREGRINE FALCON	GORILLA
BLACK-FOOTED FERRET	BROWN HYENA	RED KANGAROO
LEMUR	MACAW	MANATEE
MANDRILL	MARGAY	SPIDER MONKEY
OCELOT	ORANGUTAN	GIANT PANDA
GALAPAGOS PENGUIN	BLACK RHINOCEROS	SOCKEYE SALMON
GOLDEN LION TAMARIN	TIGER	GALAPAGOS TORTOISE
WALLABY	BLUE WHALE	GRAY WOLF

Use the index volume of an encyclopedia to help you find information about each of your three animals. Below, write something interesting about each animal.

★ ____

____

★ ____

____

★ ____

____

Choose one animal for further research. Use an encyclopedia and science reference books to learn about your animal. Take notes on a separate sheet of paper. Imagine you are your endangered animal. Use what you have learned to complete the interview on the next page.

Name ______________________________

ENDANGERED INTERVIEW, CONTINUED

INTERVIEWER: We are here today with ____________________, an endangered animal. Please tell our audience what you look like.

ANIMAL: ______________________________

____

INTERVIEWER: Where is your home?

ANIMAL: ______________________________

____

INTERVIEWER: What do you do there?

ANIMAL: ______________________________

____

INTERVIEWER: What do you like to eat?

ANIMAL: ______________________________

____

INTERVIEWER: Why are you endangered?

ANIMAL: ______________________________

____

INTERVIEWER: What is being done to help you and your kind?

ANIMAL: ______________________________

____

INTERVIEWER: What would you most like people to know about you?

ANIMAL: ______________________________

____

Do any endangered animals live near your home?

When you have finished writing your interview, ask a friend to be the interviewer. Practice the interview, with your friend reading the part of the interviewer and you being your animal. Perform your interview for your class or tape it on audiotape to listen to later!

Name ______________________

ANIMAL PRODUCTS

Are you wearing shoes with leather on them? Did you eat eggs or meat today? Leather, eggs, and meat are animal products. Many products we use every day come from animals. Some people don't think we should use any animal products. Many people think we should look for alternatives to the products that come from animals, but what if there are no alternatives?

Today you will talk about some animal products. You will discuss your ideas with a group of at least three other people. After your group shares its ideas, you will consider the discussion and reach some conclusions of your own.

Think about each animal product listed. If you are not sure what a product is, be sure to find out. Consider whether such use harms the animal. Is there any reasonable alternative? How important is this product to human life? Share your ideas with your group. Be sure that everyone in the group has a chance to speak. Make notes for and against the use of each animal product.

Complete each sentence by telling what each product is. Then make notes of arguments for and against each use.

AMBERGRIS is ______________________

____

for:

against:

WOOL is ______________________

____

for:

against:

Name________________________________

ANIMAL PRODUCTS, CONTINUED

INSULIN is ____

____

for: **against:**

IVORY is ____

____

for: **against:**

GELATIN is ____

____

for: **against:**

FUR is ____

____

for: **against:**

Complete the questions below on your own. Your answers DO NOT need to agree with your group.

Choose one product from the list that you believe should be used and explain why you believe this.

____

____

Choose one product from the list that you believe should not be used and explain why you believe this.

____

____

What animal products are used in other parts of the world?

Name ______________________________

EXOTIC INVADERS

In 1869 a scientist in Massachusetts was studying the gypsy moth. Accidentally, some of the moths were released. Until that time, gypsy moths lived only in Europe and Asia. The moth had no natural enemies in North America.

The gypsy moths reproduced quickly in their new environment. Soon gypsy moths spread throughout New England. Today gypsy moth caterpillars are destroying forests as far away as Oregon and California.

The gypsy moth is what scientists call an "exotic invader." It is an animal that is not native to the environment. Often these exotic invaders are moved from place to place by people—usually accidentally, but sometimes on purpose. Because the invaders have no natural enemies, they spread quickly. Usually they become serious pests. Often invaders crowd out or kill off native species.

People are becoming more aware of the problems that exotic invaders cause. Many countries and states restrict what animals and plants may cross their borders. They hope to keep out exotic invaders.

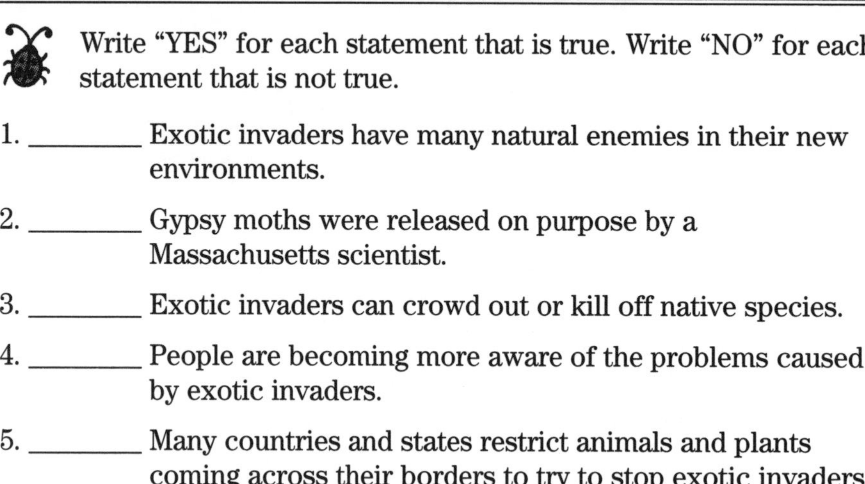

Write "YES" for each statement that is true. Write "NO" for each statement that is not true.

1. ________ Exotic invaders have many natural enemies in their new environments.
2. ________ Gypsy moths were released on purpose by a Massachusetts scientist.
3. ________ Exotic invaders can crowd out or kill off native species.
4. ________ People are becoming more aware of the problems caused by exotic invaders.
5. ________ Many countries and states restrict animals and plants coming across their borders to try to stop exotic invaders.

Choose one of the animal invaders listed below. See what you can find out about this animal's invasion. Where did it come from? How did it travel so far? What have been the effects of its invasion on its new environment? Make notes of your findings on the back of this sheet. Share your information with the rest of your class.

Zebra mussel	African (killer) honeybee
Sea lamprey	European starling
Asiatic freshwater clam	Common carp
Feral pig	Cannibal snail

Name______________________________

AN ANIMAL PUZZLE

carnivore
cow
bear
animals
marine
mammal
marsupials
primate
camel
killer whale
chimpanzee
monkey
baboon
rodent

ACROSS

2. the "moo" animal
3. whale, dolphin, or seal
5. marine mammal; orca
8. the grizzly ________
9. a mammal like man
10. desert animal
11. mouse, beaver, or rat

DOWN

1. meat eater
2. ape most like man
3. pouched mammals
4. small primate
6. hoofed ________
7. dog-like primate

ANIMAL LIFE SPANS

Name ______________________________

Use the time line at the bottom of this page to help you answer these questions.

1. How long do horses live? ________ years

2. How long do humans live? ________

3. Which animals live longer than a lion? ____________________

____

4. Which animal lives for an average of 13 years? ____________________

5. Which animals have life spans that are shorter than a bear? ____________________

____

Use subtraction to help you answer these questions about the animals on the time line.

WORK SPACE

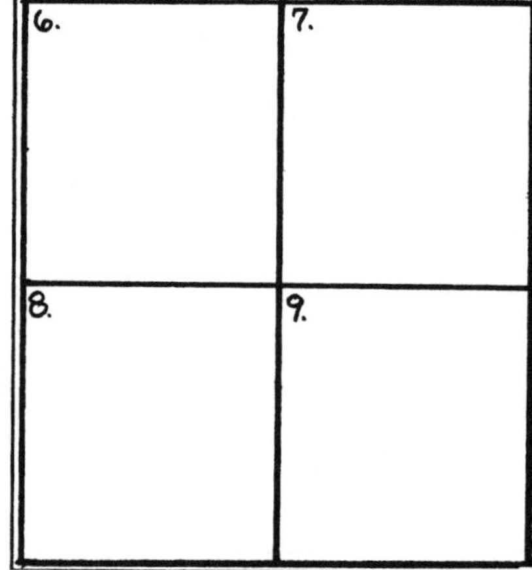

6. How much longer will a person live than a hippopotomus? ________ years

7. How many years longer do chimpanzees live than dogs? ____________________

8. How much longer is a cat's life span than the life of a mouse? ____________________

9. How much shorter is the life span of a lion than that of an elephant? ______________

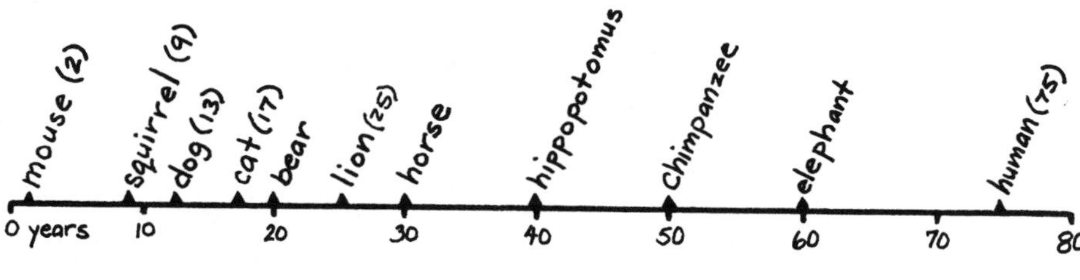

Name________________________________

ANIMAL QUICK CHECK

Use the word box to help you complete the sentences.

zoologists	adapt	decomposers	domestic	niche
extinct	phylum	habitat	carnivore	camouflage

1. Animals change or ______________________ to suit their environment.
2. Scientists who study animals are called ______________________.
3. Animals need food, water, and a safe ______________________ where they can raise their young.
4. ______________________ animals are tame animals that are raised by people.
5. A ______________________ is a classification or grouping of animals.
6. ______________________ and scavengers return nutrients to the soil while they clean the environment.
7. Each animal species fills a certain ______________________ in the ecosystem.

Write "YES" for true and "NO" for not true.

8. _________ All animals need the oxygen that plants produce in photosynthesis.
9. _________ Animals are classified by common characteristics and habits.
10. _________ To win the battle for survival, animals need only food and a place to raise their young.
11. _________ Animals defend themselves and their young in many ways
12. _________ Every plant and animal in an ecosystem is important.
13. _________ Animals are the only producers in the food chain.
14. _________ Animal invaders do little damage in their new environmen

Scientists have classified more than 1,000,000 different animal species... so far!

★ Think about the most interesting or important thing you h learned about animals. Write about it on the back of this s...

Name ___________________________

A WORD SEARCH ABOUT PEOPLE

Circle each of the words you find in the word search. The words can be found either down or across.

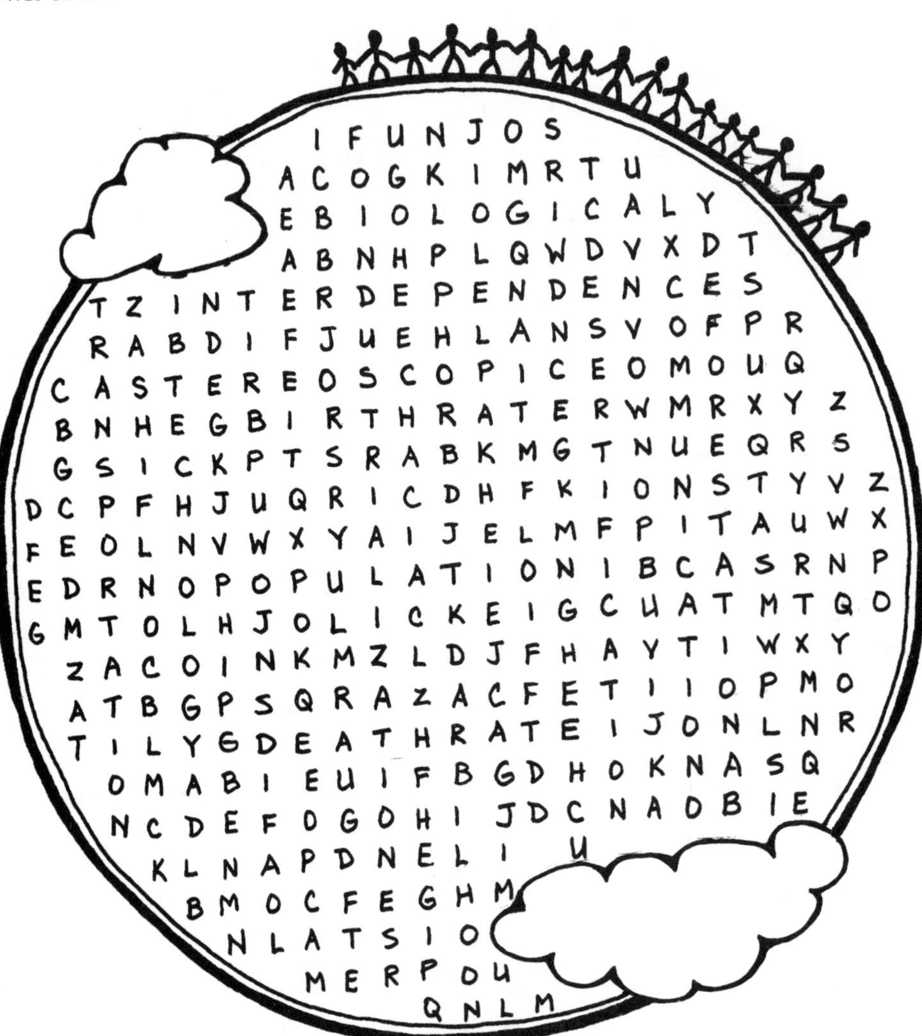

BIOLOGICAL	TRANSPORTATION	STEREOSCOPIC	DEFORESTATION
TECHNOLOGY	INTERDEPENDENCE	COMMUNICATION	DEATH RATE
BIRTH RATE	DESERTIFICATION	INDUSTRIALIZATION	POPULATION

Name________________________________

PEOPLE HANDWRITING

People have more impact on the environment than any other creature.

culture

traditions

flexible

adaptable

civilization

unique

opposable

upright

curious

habitat

Name ______________________________

A LITTLE HISTORY

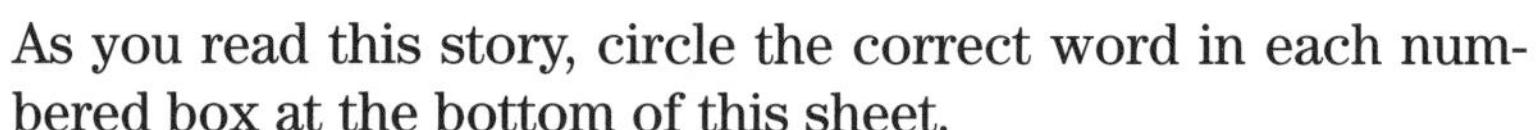

As you read this story, circle the correct word in each numbered box at the bottom of this sheet.

People have been calling the earth home for at least a couple of million years. We are highly intelligent and 1.__________ adaptable creatures. What have we been doing for all those years?

Most scientists agree that the earliest 2.__________ were busy hunting and gathering food. To find enough to 3.__________, small groups of people moved from place to place. They hunted 4.__________ and searched for wild edible plants. Everyone in the group—adults and children—were involved in securing 5.____________. This way of life continued for probably two million years.

About 10,000 years ago people discovered agriculture. They learned that 6.___________ seeds and raising useful animals were good ways to keep food available. People who planted 7.____________ stayed in one place. They didn't need to travel around looking for 8.____________ all the time. Something else happened around this time. People found that growing food took less time and produced much more than 9.____________ and gathering.

More available food meant that more people could live together in one place. Not everyone needed to 10.___________ at securing food. People developed governments, arts, and sciences. Advanced civilizations and complex cultures grew around the world.

About 300 years ago people learned to use fossil fuels, such as coal and oil, to run machines. Industry and technology have advanced quickly. This "industrial revolution" has contributed to most of today's environmental challenges. We have come so far. Now is the time to decide what our future will be.

There are still people who live by hunting and gathering.

1.	2.	3.	4.	5.
highly poorly not	animals plants people	eat waste bury	plants soil animals	groups people food
6. losing cooking planting	**7.** animals crops agriculture	**8.** soil food animals	**9.** gathering hunting planting	**10.** discover work travel

Name______________________________

A LITTLE CULTURE

As you read this story, circle the correct word in each numbered box at the bottom of this sheet.

People everywhere have the same biological needs. We all need food, 1.____________, and homes. You probably don't eat much octopus. You rarely 2.___________ flowing robes to school or sleep in a thatch hut. These are common in some parts of the 3.____________. Why are people's habits and ways of life so different? The 4._____________ is culture.

In different parts of the world, people have learned 5.____________ ways to survive. These different, learned behaviors are cultural. Every human being needs to eat. That 6.____________ a biological need. How we eat, what we eat, and when we eat are all 7.______________ of our culture.

Culture is learned ways of thinking, feeling, and acting. These include language, religion, 8.______________, and traditions. Culture is so much a part of us that we sometimes think our 9.____________ of doing things is the best way or only way. We are most comfortable with people who share our culture.

Culture changes and adapts to new information and ideas. Ask your 10.___________ about changes in food, clothes, and music since they were children. More than ever, people are learning about other cultures. Modern transportation and communication have made us more aware of our differences and similarities. We can learn from each other.

Our culture influences how we view our natural environment. The Native American culture is closely tied to the interdependence of man and the earth. Its custom and traditions embrace the environment. The cultures of most developed nations are just beginning to consider our impact on the earth.

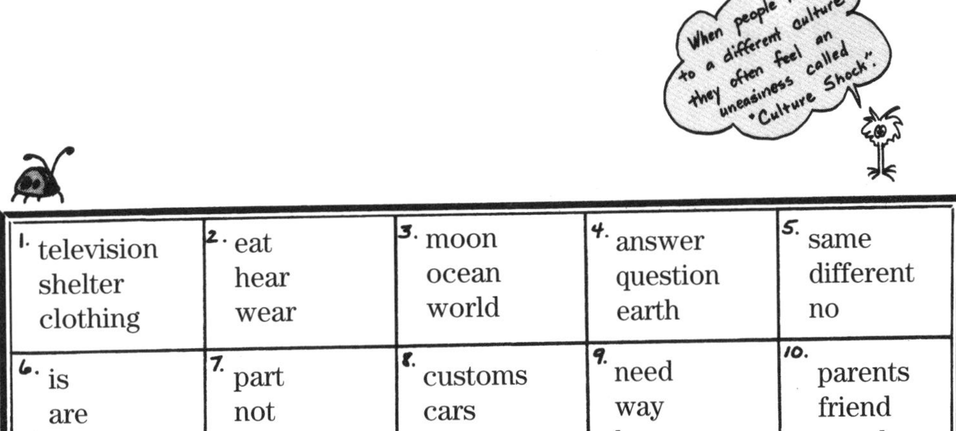

1.	2.	3.	4.	5.
television shelter clothing	eat hear wear	moon ocean world	answer question earth	same different no
6. is are were	**7.** part not different	**8.** customs cars common	**9.** need way learn	**10.** parents friend people

Name ______________________________

WE ARE UNIQUE

Ready:

1. Something that is "one of a kind" is said to be __________________.

unique opposable intricate grasp upright adaptable flexible curious complex stereoscopic

2. __________________ is a compound word.

3. Two words that mean something can change easily are __________________ and __________________.

4. A person who wants to know everything is__________________.

5. __________________ comes from the root word "opposite."

6. Two words that mean complicated are __________________ and __________________.

People and other animals have many things in common. We have, basically, the same needs as other animals. People need clean air and water. We need food and shelter. Both animals and people must have safe places to raise their young.

The earth is home to more than 20 million species. Among all species, people are unique. We have many special abilities that are ours alone. Our brains are twice as large as the brains of our nearest relatives, the apes.

We have large eyes that are set in the front of our skulls. This gives us stereoscopic vision. That means we can see depth or how near or far something is.

People, like apes and monkeys, have opposable thumbs. Our hands can grasp and hold. They are highly developed and very sensitive. We can perform the most intricate manual tasks.

Name________________________________

WE ARE UNIQUE, CONTINUED

The curve in our lower spines make it possible for us to stand erect.

Our hands are even more useful because we stand upright. People walk on two feet. This frees our hands to carry and handle objects.

Human beings are the most adaptable of all creatures. We live everywhere on the earth and have even traveled to the moon. People have great flexibility and participate in a great variety of behavior. We are also extraordinarily curious. We seem to be born with an overpowering need to find out—everything!

People have one characteristic that makes us truly unique. That characteristic is speech. We can talk! People can communicate very complex ideas. We can even record our ideas for future generations—through writing.

You can pick up a book and share an idea of someone who lived 1000 years ago. You can write a letter and send your ideas to a friend across the continent. It is through the development of language that our culture is passed along from generation to generation. Written language makes it possible for us to learn the lessons of the past without making the same studies and mistakes that other people have already made.

Language, combined with our curiosity and ability to learn and change our behavior have set human beings apart from other animals. These abilities make it possible for us to choose our future. We are unique.

Go:

1. People and animals share basic needs for ____________, ______________, ________________, and ______________.

2. Our brains are (smaller, larger) than other animals.

3. Our large eyes in the front of our skull give us ______________ vision.

4. We have ______________ that are opposable and help our hands perform intricate tasks.

5. People are the most adaptable of all animals. (YES, NO)

6. What is our most unique characteristic and why does it make us unique? ______________

____

____

Name ________________________________

WORLD POPULATION GROWTH

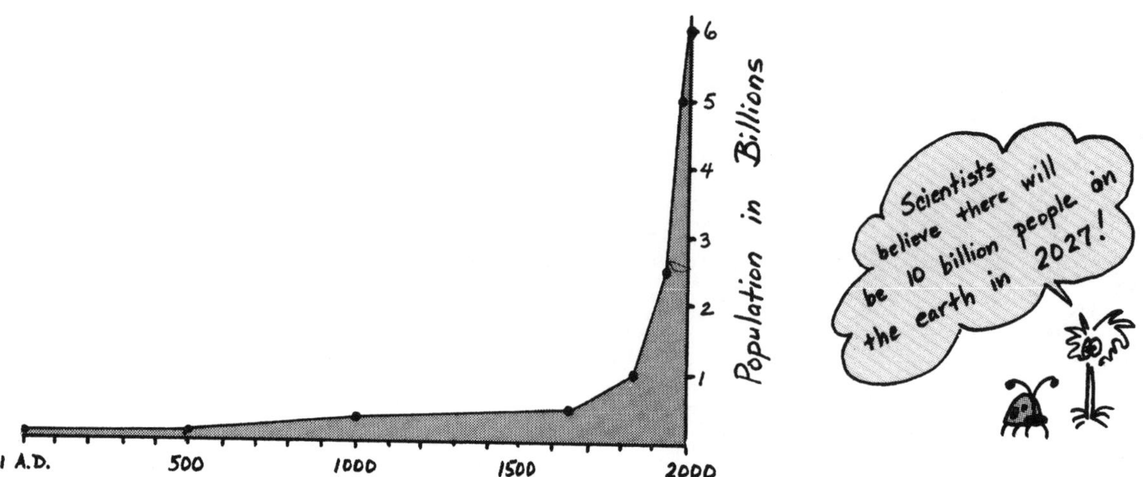

In 1800 most North American families lived on farms. The average family had seven children. There were many good things about large families. Children helped with the farm work. Also health care was poor. Having many children increased the chance that some would live to grow up. Adult children would care for their parents in old age.

Today the average family in industrialized countries has two children. Machines do much of our work and few families live on farms. We have better health care and vaccines to prevent many childhood diseases. The rate of population growth in industrialized nations is small.

In many underdeveloped countries, women still have many children. Because of improvements in food production and health care, more of these children live long enough to have children of their own. The population growth rate in most underdeveloped countries is high.

You share the world with more than 5.4 billion people. The world's population is bigger than it has ever been and it is growing every day. In fact, many people find the growth in population alarming. In less than 10 years scientists believe we will add another billion people to the planet.

When you get into your bed tonight, there will be 250,000 more people in the world than when you got up. Every day about 400,000 babies are born. Each day about 150,000 people die. The difference in the birth rate and the death rate is the population growth.

Name ______________________________

WORLD POPULATION GROWTH, CONTINUED

About 2,000 years ago the world's population was about 1 million people. It took nearly 1,000 years to double that number. By 1825 people were doubling the population every 100 years. At our present rate we will have twice as many people on the earth in just 35 years!

90% of the world's population growth is in the poorest countries.

Use the information in the article to help you answer these questions.

1. How many people live on the earth? __________ billion

2. How long do scientists think it will take to add another billion people to our population?

   __________ years

3. If the birth rate is higher than the death rate, what happens to the population? __________

4. What were the advantages of having large families? __________

5. What two advances have caused the population to grow so quickly? __________

Why do you think smaller families are better for our environment? __________

Name ______________________________

WHERE ARE ALL THE PEOPLE?

Land areas cover more than 57 million square miles of the earth's surface. Today our human population would average about 95 people per square mile—if we were evenly spaced around the world. However, we are not distributed evenly. People are bunched up in pockets of large population.

If you look at a population map, you will see that many people live in some areas while other places have few people. If we are getting crowded, why don't we just spread out? Some locations are more desirable for people to live than others. People live where it is easiest to meet their basic needs.

About 10,000 years ago people learned to farm. Flat, fertile land with few trees was easiest to farm. People settled in areas with flat, fertile land. Later, as people learned to trade with other groups, transportation became important. Cities grew up near good water transportation routes. Physical features of the earth, like mountains and rivers, strongly influenced where people settled. Today most people still live on flat, fertile plains near major water transportation.

How people make a living influences where they live. In the early 1800's most people lived on farms. As farming advanced and produced more food, fewer farms were needed to feed the population. Now most of the people on the earth live in cities. Climate also influences where people live. Many parts of the earth are just too cold, too wet, or too mountainous to attract many people.

Name ________________________________

WHERE ARE ALL THE PEOPLE?, CONTINUED

Actually, only a small part of the earth's surface is well suited to humans. People are already living in just about all of the best places. As our population grows, people are using more and more land that is not well suited for people. This causes more and more harm to these fragile areas. Scientists believe this is putting a strain on all of our natural environment.

Write "YES" for each true statement. Write "NO" for each statement that is not true.

1. _______ Population is evenly distributed around the world.
2. _______ People settled on flat, fertile plains because the land was good for farming.
3. _______ Few people lived near large bodies of water.
4. _______ Climate influences where people choose to live.
5. _______ People are already living in nearly all of the most desirable places.

Think about each of the features listed below. Decide if you would like to live near each feature or not. Tell why or why not.

6. STEEP MOUNTAINS ____

____

7. A LARGE CITY ____

____

8. LARGE FACTORIES ____

____

9. HEAVY FORESTS ____

____

10. AN AIRPORT ____

____

11. A SMALL TOWN ____

____

Name ________________________________

WHAT ARE WE DOING?

deforestation
impact
endless
resources
population
grassland
desertification
habitat
behavior
industrialized

1. The word ________________________ is a compound word.
2. The natural area where species live is called their ________________________.
3. Something that has an effect on something else has an ________________________ on it.
4. The one word from the list that has six syllables is ________________________.
5. The ________________________ of an area is the number of people living there.

People have a greater impact on the earth than any other animal. Our search for food, water, and shelter has changed the face of the earth. Further, we have a seemingly endless desire for goods and services beyond our basic needs. More cars, televisions, and other consumer goods are produced every day. There are also more people on the earth every day. More people wanting more things are straining the earth's resources.

In many parts of the world most people still live by farming. These areas also have rapidly growing populations. People are cutting down or burning forests to make more farm land. Deforestation doesn't work very well because the forest soil is poor. The soil soon wears out and more forest is destroyed to replace the exhausted land.

Name________________________________

WHAT ARE WE DOING?, CONTINUED

In warm, dry, grassland areas people raise cattle, sheep, and goats. As grazing areas become crowded the animals eat nearly all the plants. When all the plants are gone, people move their animals to a new place. Without plants to hold the soil, desertification takes place. Deserts grow and grasslands become smaller. More animals grazing a smaller area makes the problem even worse.

Growing human populations take up more and more space. Wildlife habitat is replaced by homes, farms, and cities. Animals have fewer places to live. People also hunt wild animals for food, hides, or sport. Many animal species are now extinct. Others are endangered or threatened by people's behavior.

More people also means more pollution. Industrialized countries are big polluters. Burning fossil fuels pollutes the air. Pesticides and landfills pollute water. We may even be causing the earth's atmosphere to warm.

Education is important if we are going to stop harming the earth. People don't hurt the earth on purpose. They are trying to care for themselves and their families. We need to work together to help everyone earn a living without damaging our environment.

The Sahara Desert is growing by 4 million acres every year!

1. People have a greater impact on the earth than any other animal. (YES, NO)

2. More people wanting more things are straining the earth's limited ________________.

3. Why isn't deforestation a good way to gain farm land?____

4. Over-grazing in warm, dry areas is causing (industrialization, deforestation, desertification).

5. How does the growing human population harm wildlife? ______________________

____

6. In industrialized countries ________________ and ______________ are becoming more polluted.

Name ______________________________

NEED OR WANT?

When is one person really ten people? The answer is when the person lives in an industrialized country, like the United States, and uses ten times as much energy and resources as a person living in an underdeveloped country. People in industrialized countries have a high standard of living. We have many products and services available. Most people enjoy all the necessities of life. Many people also have a wide variety of luxury items.

Many people believe we must learn to live more simply if we are to save our natural environment. They want all of us to think about what we really need and what we just want to have.

Today you will think and talk about some common products. You will share ideas with a group of at least three other people. Then you will think about and answer some of the questions on your own.

Look at the list below. Next to each item that you think is a necessity of life or a basic need, write "N." If the item is a luxury or not really needed to live, write "L."

__________ stereo

__________ car

__________ bicycle

__________ clean water

__________ blankets

__________ athletic shoes

__________ microwave oven

__________ clothes

__________ television

__________ fruit

__________ electric lights

__________ bread

__________ house

__________ paper

__________ meat

__________ jacket

Discuss these items in your group. You may change your answers, if you wish, but you do NOT have to agree with everyone in your group.

Name________________________________

NEED OR WANT?, CONTINUED

Look at the items on the list that all of your group members agreed were luxury items. Discuss with your group and list the luxuries in order of importance. Make the most important luxury "1." The next most important luxury will be "2." Continue until you have listed all the items your group agreed were luxury items.

____

____

____

____

____

Compare your group's list with the lists of other groups. Discuss any differences. Have any of your opinions changed?

____

____

____

Think about one product you use that you believe is a luxury. It can be from the list or something else. How would your life be different if you used this luxury or didn't have it at all? How would the environment change if you used less of this luxury?

____

____

____

____

____

____

Name ______________________________

PEOPLE AND RESOURCES

People use the earth's natural resources for food, fuel, and raw materials. Our food comes from plant and animal sources. We use oil, coal, and natural gas for fuel. We use many kinds of natural resources for industry to produce everything from steel beams to plastic grocery bags.

Today you will research and learn about some of the natural resources people use. Use an encyclopedia, your science or social studies textbooks, or other sources to help you gather information. Find out what each resource is, where it is found, and what people do with it.

For each resource listed, write at least three sentences:

- Tell what the resource is and where it is found.
- Tell how the resource is used by people.
- Tell how we might be affected if this resource was no longer available.

BAUXITE ______________________________

____

____

____

WOOD PULP ______________________________

____

____

____

SAND ______________________________

____

____

____

Name ____________________

PEOPLE AND RESOURCES, CONTINUED

PETROLEUM ____________________

LEATHER ____________________

IRON ____________________

COAL ____________________

RUBBER ____________________

COTTON ____________________

On the back of this sheet, make a list of other natural resources that people use. See how many you can find.

Name ______________________________

SURPRISE SLOGAN

We have learned much about our environment. We are a part of a complex interdependency. Our own earth is the perfect habitat for us. Many smart people are helping to save our home.

There is a hidden message in the paragraph above. Follow these directions carefully to find the surprise slogan.

1. Cross out every other word in the paragraph.
2. Now cross out every other remaining word.
3. Then cross out every other word still remaining in the paragraph.
4. Circle the four words that you did not cross out.
5. Write the surprise slogan on the flag below. Decorate and color your flag.

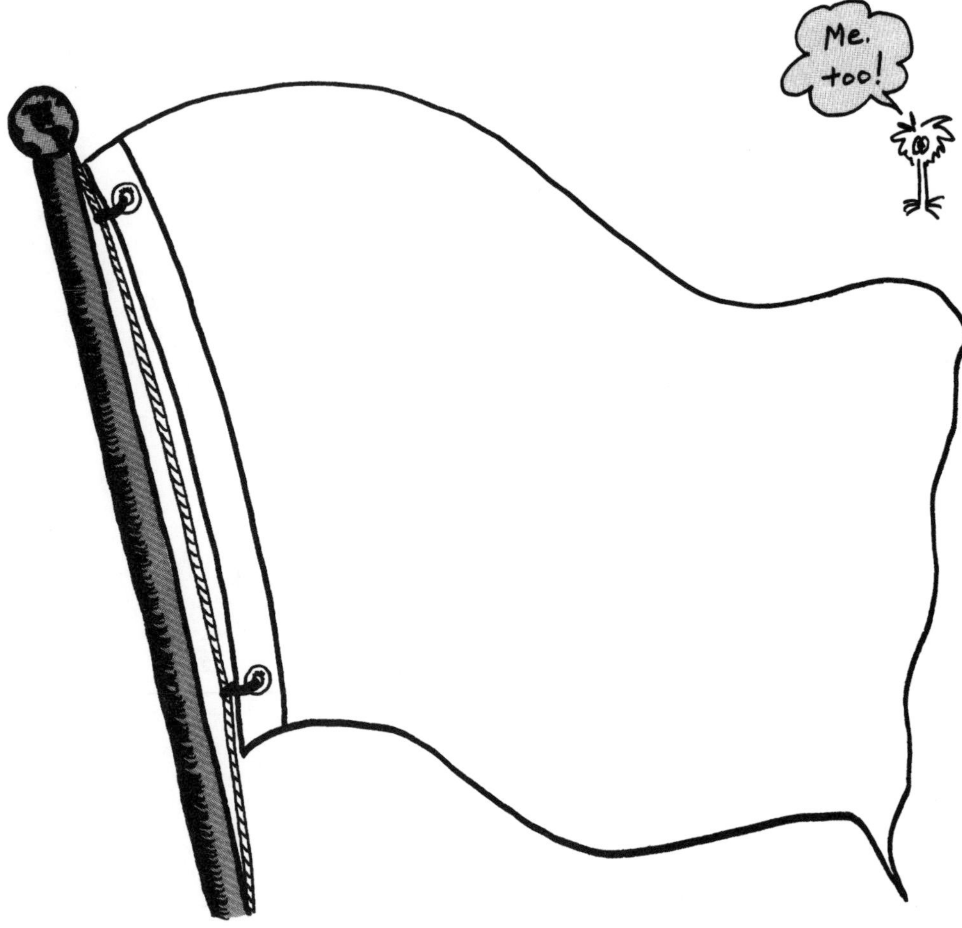

Name________________________________

CLASSROOM SQUEEZE

Look around your classroom. Now imagine that the class next to yours must share your classroom. You now have twice as many people sharing the same space. What about desks, chairs, and other supplies?

The earth is like your classroom. There is only so much food, water, and space to go around. The more people, the further our limited resources must stretch.

Think again about your classroom space. Another class joins you. They can't bring anything with them. You must share what you have with the newcomers—including your lunch! Below, tell what you think your experience would be like. Consider what problems might come up. What about noise? Could there be disagreements? Who decides how to share scarce supplies? If this arrangement is permanent, how will it effect your education?

Remember—there will be twice as many people in just 35 years!

____

____

____

____

____

____

____

____

____

____

____

____

Name ______________________________

LIFE EXPECTANCY

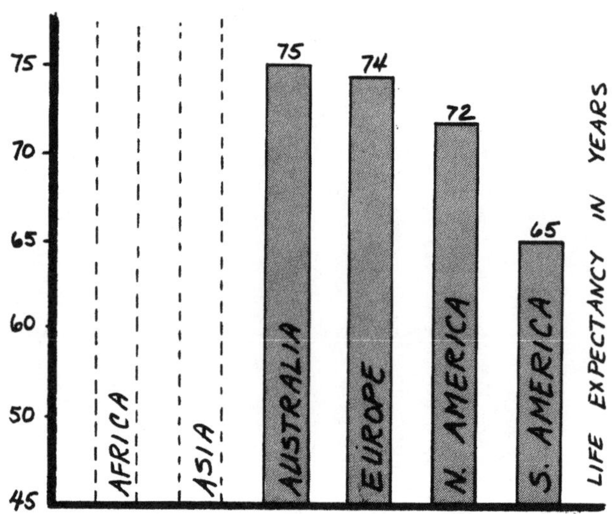

How long a person will live is influenced by many things. One factor seems to be where you live. The graph shows the average life expectancy on four continents: Australia, Europe, North America, and South America. The life expectancy for Asia is 60 years. The life expectancy for Africa is 50 years.

Why isn't Antarctica on the list?

Graph the life expectancies of Africa and Asia in the spaces provided. Then use the graph to help you answer the questions below.

WORK SPACE

1. How much longer does the average person in Australia live than the average person in Africa?

   ______________________________ years.

2. How much longer does the average person in North America live than the average person in Asia?

   ____

3. How much longer does the average person in Europe live than the average person in South America?

   ____

4. List the continents in the order of their life expectancies. Make the continent with the shortest life expectancy first. ______________________________

____

____

____

Name________________________________

PEOPLE QUICK CHECK

Use the word box to help you complete the sentences.

culture	opposable	industrialization	habitat	unique
deforestation	population	agriculture	language	biological

1. People have _____________ thumbs that enable us to perform intricate tasks.
2. About 10,000 years ago people discovered ___________ and began to raise their own food.
3. _____________ is learned ways of thinking, feeling, and acting.
4. Special characteristics and abilities make us ______________ among animals.
5. Our use of ____________ sets us apart from other species.
6. The earth's ______________ is more than 5.4 billion people.
7. _____________ occurs when people clear forests to use the land for other purposes.

Write "YES" for true and "NO" for not true.

What is another name for Earth? HOME!

8. ________ People are the least adaptable of all creatures on the earth.
9. ________ Agriculture allowed people to develop advanced civilizations.
10. ________ Modern transportation and communication have made it more difficult to learn about other cultures.
11. ________ We have little in common with other animals because our basic needs are so different.
12. ________ Population growth rates are lowest in underdeveloped countries.
13. ________ The people of the world are evenly distributed over the earth's surface.
14. ________ Physical features of the earth strongly influence where people choose to live.

★ Think about the most interesting thing you have learned about people and the environment. Write about it on the back of this sheet.

Ecology Notes

SECTION FOUR

CONSERVATION

WHAT CAN WE DO?

Name ______________________________

AN ENERGY WORD SEARCH

Circle each of the words you find in the word. The words can be found either down or across.

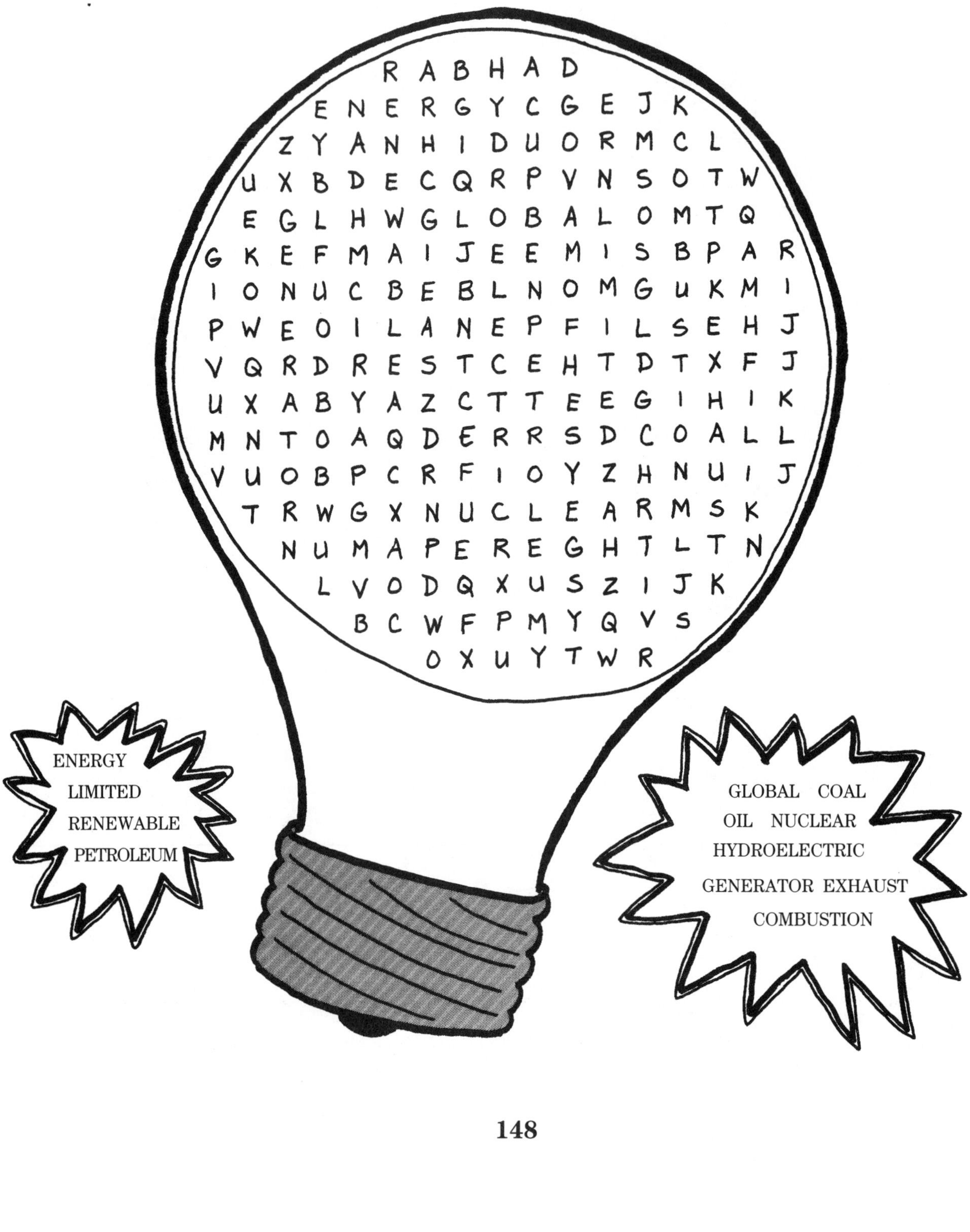

R A B H A D
E N E R G Y C G E J K
Z Y A N H I D U O R M C L
U X B D E C Q R P V N S O T W
E G L H W G L O B A L O M T Q
G K E F M A I J E E M I S B P A R
I O N U C B E B L N O M G U K M I
P W E O I L A N E P F I L S E H J
V Q R D R E S T C E H T D T X F J
U X A B Y A Z C T T E E G I H I K
M N T O A Q D E R R S D C O A L L
V U O B P C R F I O Y Z H N U I J
T R W G X N U C L E A R M S K
N U M A P E R E G H T L T N
L V O D Q X U S Z I J K
B C W F P M Y Q V S
O X U Y T W R

ENERGY
LIMITED
RENEWABLE
PETROLEUM

GLOBAL COAL
OIL NUCLEAR
HYDROELECTRIC
GENERATOR EXHAUST
COMBUSTION

Name________________________________

ENERGY HANDWRITING

fossil fuel ________________________________

____

transportation ________________________________

____

machines ________________________________

____

appliances ________________________________

____

sulfur dioxide ________________________________

____

alternative ________________________________

____

natural gas ________________________________

____

fission ________________________________

____

radioactive ________________________________

____

electricity ________________________________

____

Name ______________________________

ENERGY FOR THE EARTH

As you read this story, circle the correct word in each numbered box at the bottom of this sheet.

Did you have some energy for breakfast this morning? If you ate cereal or 1.__________ orange juice, you were actually consuming 2.____________. The food you eat is changed into energy in your body. You 3.________ energy to play, work, and grow.

Where did the energy come from in the 4.__________ place? All of the earth's energy comes from the sun. The 5.__________ energy is used by plants to make food in a process called photosynthesis. In this way plants 6.___________ energy for their use and ours. Energy is stored in the food we eat. Energy is 7.___________ in the wood we burn. Over millions and millions of years energy has been stored in fossil 8.___________ like oil and coal. These fuels are very important for industry and transportation.

We use energy to keep warm, do work, and move people and things from place to place. Most 9._________ take energy so much for granted that they only notice when energy stops flowing. Think about the last time your electricity was out. You probably were surprised at how 10.______________ things you were forced to do without. Did you automatically try to turn on the lights when you went into a room, even though you knew there was no power? The use of energy has become habit to most of us.

Because we are so dependent on energy, it makes sense to learn all we can about it. Learning about energy and its uses will help us make wise choices about our own use of this valuable resource.

The sun beams down 20,000 times as much energy as we need!

1.	2.	3.	4.	5.
ate drank left	animals energy juice	need want waste	last first once	sun's moon's tide's
6.	**7.**	**8.**	**9.**	**10.**
store lose eat	eaten juice stored	food animal fuels	plants people foods	many any fine

Name____________________________

MORE AND MORE ENERGY

As you read this story, circle the correct word in each numbered box at the bottom of this sheet.

About 90% of all the energy we use each day comes from fossil fuels. Our demand for these 1.__________ is growing at what some experts feel is an alarming rate. Before 1900 we 2.__________ only a small amount of coal, oil, or gas. Since that time the demand for 3.__________ fuels has doubled every 20 years.

There are many reasons why we are using 4.__________ and more fossil fuels. One reason is simply that there are so many more 5.__________ in our rapidly growing population. More people need more jobs. Most of these jobs use 6.__________ to produce things. People have more wealth than ever before. They want many 7.__________ that require energy to produce.

One of the most important reasons for the increase in 8.__________ use is machines. Since about 1850, scientists have invented an incredible number of machines. These inventions do every kind of human work. They can do everything from cook your food to dry your 9.__________.

These inventions, from cars to televisions, use energy. They take energy to run, but a large 10.__________ of energy is also used to produce them. Producing one car uses more fuel than that car will burn in its first year on the road. The automobile is one of the largest users of fossil fuels.

Americans drive more than one <u>trillion</u> miles every year. Are all those trips really necessary?

Fossil fuels are also used to make plastics, nylon, pesticides synthetic rubber...

1.	2.	3.	4.	5.
uses people fuels	used lost had	these their then	less many more	people fuels fossils
6.	**7.**	**8.**	**9.**	**10.**
energy double fossils	energy fuels things	things these energy	ears hands feet	reason need amount

Name ______________________________

FOSSIL FUELS

fossil fuels petroleum prehistoric remains pressure supply global drought failure sulfuric acid

1. The word with the root word "history" is ________________.
2. An adjective that means "having to do with the whole earth" is ________________________.
3. When too little rain falls in an area to support normal plant growth, there is a ______________________.
4. A crop ________________ happens when some force ruins an agricultural crop.
5. Oil is another word for ________________________.
6. Acid rain contains ___________________________.

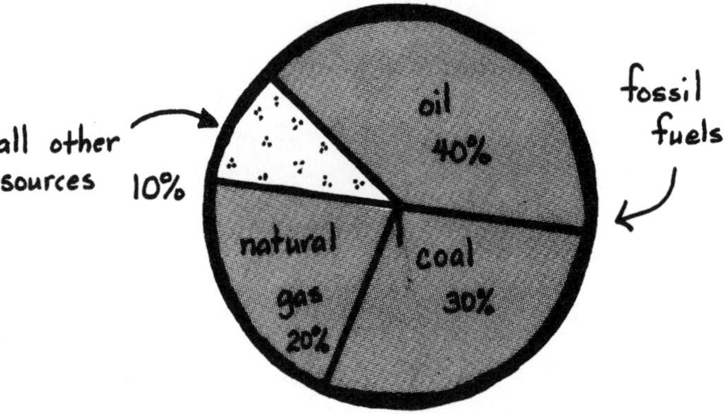

Since the industrial revolution in the 1700's and 1800's, people have doubled their demand for power every 20 years. Where does all of that energy come from? About 90% of our power comes from fossil fuels. Petroleum, coal, and natural gas are fossil fuels. These fuels are formed from prehistoric plant and animal remains. Millions of years of heat and pressure in the earth changed the plant and animal materials into oil, coal, and gas. The problem is that we are rapidly using up what took millions of years to create.

Scientists do not agree about when our supply of fossil fuels will run out. Some people think we will have used up all of the fossil fuels on earth in less than 50 years. Other scientists believe that our supply of fossil fuels will last more than 100 years. All scientists agree on one thing. We will run out of fossil fuels. They are a limited resource. When all the oil, coal, and natural gas are gone, there will be no more available for our use.

Name________________________________

FOSSIL FUELS, CONTINUED

Fossil fuels cause a variety of environmental problems. Even if the supply of these fuels were unlimited, there are some very good reasons to use less. Burning fossil fuels releases carbon dioxide into the air. The build-up of carbon dioxide can increase the greenhouse effect in the earth's atmosphere. Scientists worry that the earth's atmosphere will get warmer, causing many climate changes around the world. Global warming could mean droughts and floods in many parts of the world. Crop failures would also be likely, leaving many people without food.

Coal contains large amounts of sulfur. When coal is burned, the sulfur is released in the air as sulfur dioxide. When the sulfur dioxide mixes with raindrops, it become sulfuric acid. This acid rain damages forests, kills fish, and erodes buildings.

We have become very dependent on fossil fuels. Many people are concerned because these resources are limited and shrinking rapidly. Using these fuels causes environmental damage. Each of us can help by finding ways to use less fossil fuels.

1. How much of the world's power comes from fossil fuels? ______________________________

The average person in India uses 0.2 kw of power each day. A person in the U.S. uses 11 kw!

2. We will always have plenty of fossil fuels available. (YES, NO)

3. Burning fossil fuels releases ______________ into the air and adds to the greenhouse effect.

4. Two things that could happen because of global warming are ______________ and ______________.

5. Burning coal releases ____________ into the air.

6. How does sulfur dioxide become acid rain? ______________________________

____

Name ______________________________

4-6 ALTERNATIVE ENERGY SOURCES

Ready:

fossil fuels
nuclear
hydroelectric
alternative
limited
solution
generator
fission
radioactive
renewable

1. Dams across rivers generate __________________ power.
2. An __________________ is used in place of something else.
3. __________________ are coal, oil, and gas.
4. Fission and fusion are both ways of generating __________________ power.
5. __________________ is the opposite of the word __________________.
6. A __________________ is a machine for making electricity.

Set:

More than 90% of the energy we use come from fossil fuels. These fuels are limited. Our supply will run out if we continue to consume fossil fuels. Many people are working to develop energy sources that will not run out. Renewable sources can be used without using them up. Some alternative energy sources are solar energy, nuclear power, and hydroelectric energy. Scientists are also working to harness the energy of the winds, waves, and tides.

The sun's rays carry 20,000 times more energy to the earth than we need. This huge amount of energy seems an easy solution to our energy problems. However, using energy directly from the sun is difficult. The sun's energy is thinly spread across all of the earth's surface. The sun's energy is also only available during the day. Collecting solar energy is also only available during the day. Collecting solar energy and having it <u>when</u> and <u>where</u> we want it is the challenge scientists face. Today, solar collectors are used to heat homes and water.

Name ______________________________

ALTERNATIVE ENERGY SOURCES, CONTINUED

Nuclear energy is being used around the world as an alternative to fossil fuels. All nuclear plants today use fission to produce electricity. Fission splits an atom to produce energy. Fission also produces radioactive waste. Radioactive waste is very dangerous and can cause sickness in people and other animals. The waste stays radioactive for thousands of years. Many people worry about storing this dangerous waste for such a long time. People are also concerned about nuclear power plant accidents. In 1986 a nuclear power plant at Chernobyl in the Soviet Union was rocked by two huge steam explosions. Radiation is still so high in that area that people will never be able to return to their homes there. Many people have died of radiation sickness.

Scientists are studying a safe way to produce nuclear energy. The new process is called fusion. Fusion combines two atoms to produce energy. Researchers believe that fusion will be clean and safe.

Hydroelectric power generates electricity when falling water turns electric generators. Hydropower is inexpensive and clean. Dams to generate hydroelectricity are built on rivers and streams. Most experts believe that nearly all of the locations good for hydropower generation are already developed. Our existing plants will continue to supply energy, but few new plants can be built. Attempts to harness tides, winds, and waves are similar to the use of hydropower. Natural forces are used to power turbines and turn electrical generators.

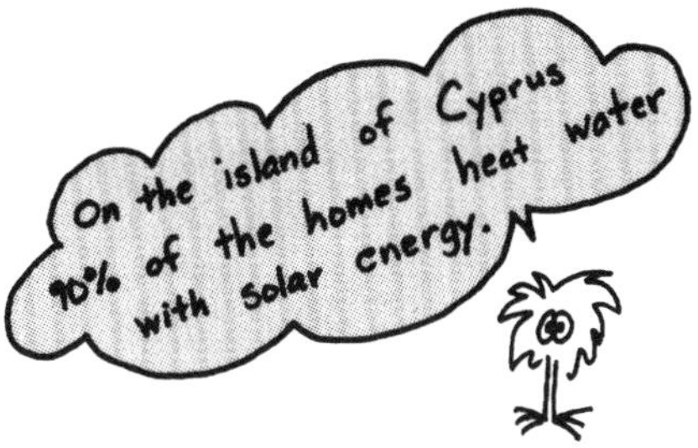

In the future, solar power, nuclear fusion, or oceans waves may be the answer to our energy needs. Today, our best immediate solution is conservation. We can use less energy today without waiting for new technology.

1. Our supply of ______________ will run out if we continue to use them.

2. Nuclear power, solar energy, and hydroelectric power are ________________ sources of energy.

3. The sun's rays carry huge amounts of energy to the earth. (YES, NO)

4. What are two problems with nuclear fission? ______________________________________

   ____

5. Beside hydropower, name two natural forces that scientists hope to harness for electrical power. _________________________ and _________________________

6. What can be done right now to reduce the use of fossil fuels? ____________________

   ____

Name ______________________________

MAKING ELECTRICITY

Electricity and magnetism are partners. This is the principle behind electric generators. Inside a generator is a magnet that spins. The spinning magnet causes electricity to flow in a wire coil that surrounds, the magnet. Power companies use steam, water, or wind to turn turbines to make the generator's magnets turns.

Steam-powered generators are the most common. Steam in these power plants is made by burning fossil fuels or by a nuclear reactor. Coal, oil, or natural gas power most steam generators.

The fuel is burned to heat a boiler. The steam from the boiler turns a turbine. A turbine is like a fan or propeller. The turbine is connected to a generator. The turbine turns the rotor or magnet inside a ring of coiled wire called the stator. Electricity flows from the stator in the generator to a transformer. The transformer concentrates the electrical power and boosts the voltage for transmission to homes and businesses.

Steam from the boiler passes through a condenser where the steam cools and changes back into liquid water. Usually the heat from this water is waste. When the heated water is returned to rivers, lakes, or streams without cooling, it causes thermal pollution. This warming of the water in the environment causes harm to plants and animals. Most areas have laws to control thermal pollution. Heated water must be cooled before it is returned to the environment. The heated water may be cooled by a spray pond or cooling tower. In some cases the hot water is even used to heat homes or businesses. In the future most of the waste heat from steam-power plants will be captured and used.

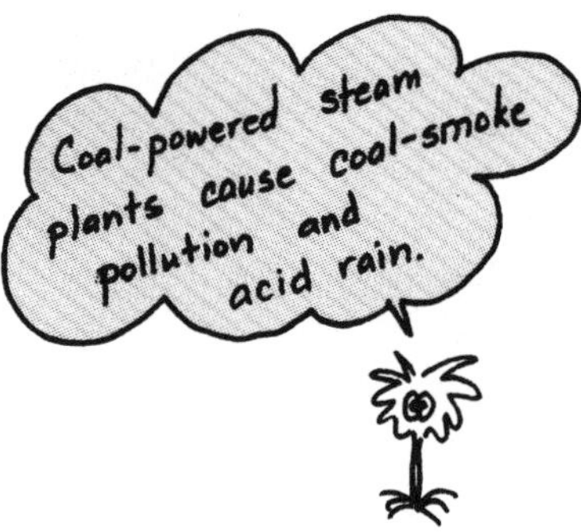

Use the underlined words from the article above to help you label the diagram of a steam electric power plant on the next page.

Name________________________

MAKING ELECTRICITY, CONTINUED

STEAM ELECTRIC POWER PLANT

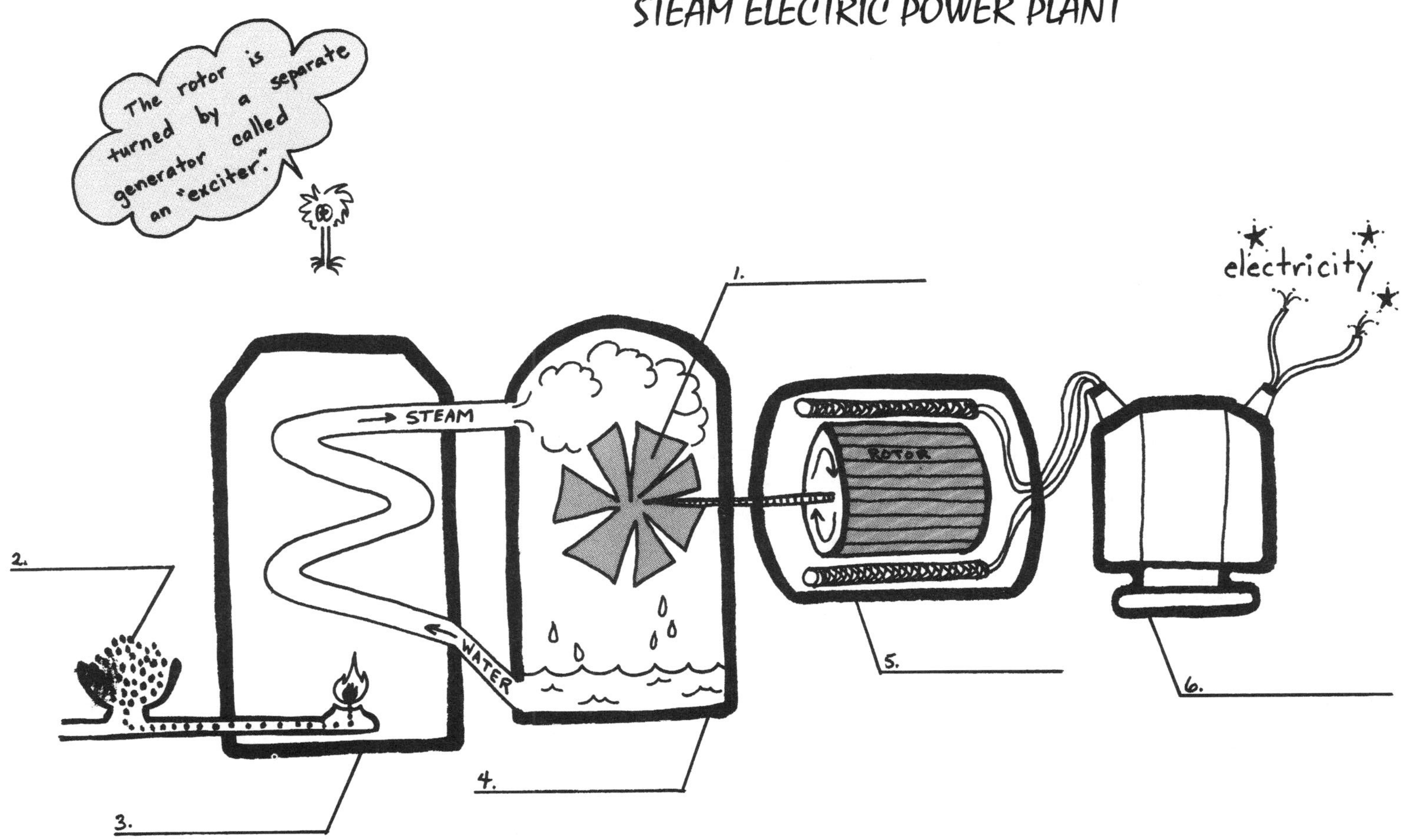

Name ______________________________

POWERFUL RESEARCH

The energy we use comes from many sources. We burn coal and oil. We build nuclear reactors to generate electricity. We have harnessed powerful rivers and strong winds. Each source of energy has advantages, but they also have disadvantages. Use an encyclopedia, science text, or other resources to find out about each energy source on the chart below.

Fill in the chart below with the information you find about each energy source. Describe each of the energy sources. Tell where each is found and whether it is limited or renewable. Explain the uses of each energy source. List the advantages and disadvantages of using each one to meet our energy demands.

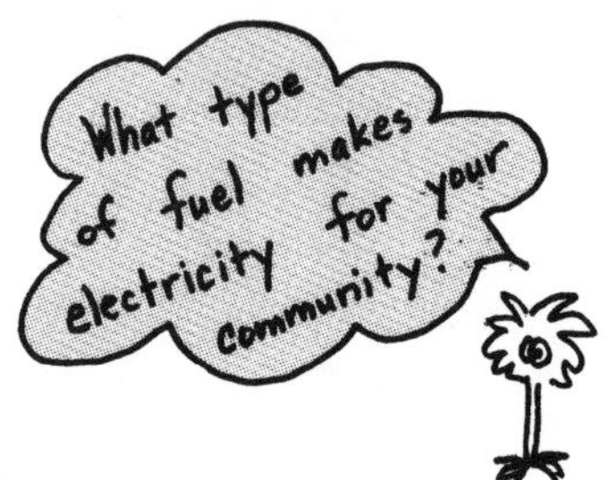

SOURCE	DESCRIPTION	USES	ADVANTAGES	DISADVANTAGES
coal				
oil				

Name______________________________

POWERFUL RESEARCH, CONTINUED

SOURCE	DESCRIPTION	USES	ADVANTAGES	DISADVANTAGES
nuclear fission				
hydro-power				
wind power				
geo-thermal power				

Name ________________________________

CARS, CARS, CARS

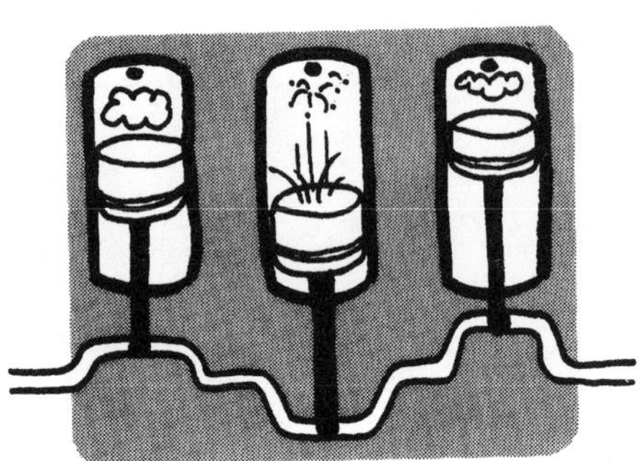

No other single invention has changed the way people live as much as the automobile. People living in industrialized countries depend on their cars for transportation to work and recreation. In North America there is one car for every two people. In the state of Florida there are more cars than people!

There are several reasons why cars have become so important. Other means of transportation, like trains, move many people to the same place at the same time. Cars let people move when and where they choose. A car gives a person independence. Cars also go door-to-door. You don't need to walk to the bus stop or train station.

The earliest automobiles were steam-powered. These "steamers" were soon replaced by gas-powered cars. Gas-powered cars use a type of motor called an internal-combustion engine. These engines burn fuel inside to create the power to drive cars. Fuel enters the engine and is ignited by a spark. Small explosions push pistons to turn a drive shaft. The shaft turns the wheels and the car moves. Smoke and fumes from the explosions leave through an exhaust pipe.

When Henry Ford produced the Model T in 1908, cars became affordable to many people. Soon most families had cars. Many families have more than one car. In fact, there are 350 million cars in the world today. In the United States alone, cars burn 125 billion gallons of gas each year. All those cars burning so much gas is damaging our environment.

Cars are one of the biggest producers of air pollution. Automobile exhaust contains carbon monoxide, hydrocarbons, and nitrogen oxides. In many communities, a car must pass a test of its exhaust in order to be licensed. If the car's emissions contain too much pollutants, the car's license cannot be renewed. Even if they did not pollute the air, cars gobble up limited fossil fuels. Many people believe that our dependence on automobiles will have to change if we are to protect our natural environment.

Name ______________________________

CARS, CARS, CARS, CONTINUED

Use the word box to help you complete these statements about cars.

trains
steam-powered
inside
explosions
pistons
choose
automobiles
affordable
engines
combustion
gas-powered
exhaust
fossil fuels
pollution
carbon dioxide

1. ______________ have changed the way people live.
2. Mass transportation, like ______________, move many people to the same place at the same time.
3. Cars let people move when and where they ______________.
4. The earliest automobiles were ______________.
5. Most cars are ______________ today.
6. Most cars' motors are internal-combustion ______________.
7. Fuel burns ______________ the car's engine.
8. Small ______________ push pistons that turn a drive shaft.
9. Smoke and fumes leave through an ______________ pipe.
10. Henry Ford made the first ______________ cars in 1908.
11. Cars are one of the biggest producers of air ______________.
12. Cars use up huge amounts of our limited supply of ______________.

How do you think we can convince people to use cars less? What might make it easier to do without so many cars?

____

____

____

____

____

Before 1900, cars were so unusual that they were exhibited in circuses!

Name ______________________________

POWERFUL DECISIONS

We use so many appliances and machines every day that we usually take them for granted. This activity will help you to think about your energy choices. You will need to work alone at home and with a group of other students at school. You will also visit with someone at least seventy years old to find out how things have changed.

Go on an energy hunt throughout your home. Make a list of every item that uses energy. Be thorough. Don't forget the portable tape player or the gas furnace or the water heater. Be sure to check the garage and the basement if you have them. When your list is complete, count the number of items. Write the total at the top of your list. Bring your list to school so you are ready to share with your group.

In a group with at least four other people, compare your lists. Circle any items that are found in at least three of your homes.

Look at the circled energy users. Discuss with your group how important each item is to you and your families. List each circled energy user under the heading below that is most appropriate. If you need more space, use the back of this sheet.

NECESSITY	USEFUL	LUXURY
______	______	______
______	______	______
______	______	______
______	______	______
______	______	______
______	______	______
______	______	______
______	______	______

Name________________________________

POWERFUL DECISIONS, CONTINUED

With your group, discuss the energy users that you listed as NECESSITIES. Number these necessities in order of importance. "1" is the most important energy user. "2" is the next most important and so on. Was this a difficult thing to do? _________ Why do you think so?

____

____

____

Talk with someone at least seventy years old. You may choose a grandparent, neighbor, or friend. Ask about the energy users from your lists. Did he/she have these things when he/she was your age? What did people use instead? How have appliances and machines changed in seventy years? Make notes on your interview here. Share your interview with your group.

I interviewed ____

Some interesting things I learned ___________________________

____

____

____

____

The lists above should tell you much about the energy you and your family use. Look at the lists and think about how you could use less energy. Tell how you and your family can save our valuable energy resources.

____

____

____

____

____

Name ______________________________

METER READER

The electricity we use is measured in watts and kilowatts. An electric meter keeps track of how many kilowatt-hours you use. A person called a meter reader visits your home regularly to note the reading on your meter.

The previous reading is subtracted from the new reading. The difference is the number of kilowatt-hours your family pays for.

An electric meter has four or five dials. The last number passed on each dial is one digit in the reading. The dial on the right is the ones digit. The next dial shows the tens digit and so on. The reading on this electric meter is 6473 kilowatt-hours.

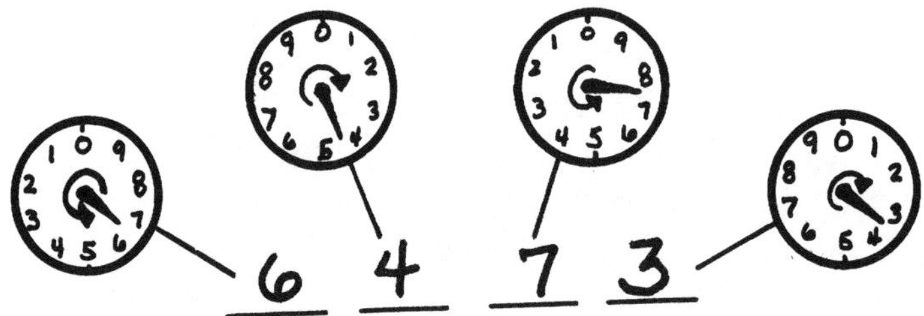

1. Read each dial on the meter below. Be careful, some of the dials turn counterclockwise. Write the digit from each dial on the correct line to show the complete meter reading.

2. The last reading on this meter was 3659 kilowatt-hours. How many kilowatt-hours has this family used?

3. Read your home electric meter. Read it again one week later. Figure out how much electricity your family has used. Compare your answers with your classmates.

WHAT R-U?

Cut out these pieces and assemble them to find out what you are.

Paste the pieces on a sheet of colored paper. Color. Decorate.

Name ______________________________

POWERFUL PROBLEMS

Use addition, subtraction, multiplication, or division to answer these "powerful" questions.

WORK SPACE

1. Each gallon of gas used by a car releases 19 pounds of carbon dioxide into the air. The average car uses about 687 gallons of gas each year. How much carbon dioxide does one car put into the air each year?

   ____

2. If you replace a 60-watt incandescent light bulb with a 15-watt florescent bulb, how many watts will you save each hour?

   ____

   If the bulb is turned on for 6 hours each day, how much energy is saved each day after the bulb is changed? __________

   How much savings in a year?

   ____

3. A standard shower head uses 7 gallons of water per minute. How much water is used for a 5-minute shower?

   ____

   An energy-saving shower head uses about 3 gallons per minute. How much water would you save on a 5-minute shower by switching to an energy-saving shower head?

   ____

4. A business has 5 outdoor security lights. Each light takes a 300-watt bulb. The lights are kept on all the time. How many watts of electricity do these lights use each day?

   ____

   If the lights were on a timer so they came on for only 12 hours per day, how much energy would be saved?

   ____

   How many watts would be saved in one year?

   ____

Name________________________

ENERGY QUICK CHECK

Use the word box to help you complete the sentences.

fossil fuels energy transportation engines heat hydroelectric prehistoric carbon dioxide fission

1. We use ______________ to keep warm, do work, and move people and things from place to place.
2. About 90% of the energy we use comes from ___________.
3. Fossil fuels formed over millions of years from _____________ plants and animals.
4. Burning fossil fuels releases ______________ into the air.
5. Nuclear ______________ produces power and radioactive waste.
6. _________________ power is generated by falling water turning a turbine.
7. Most cars use gas-powered, internal combustion _________________.

Write "YES" for true and "NO" for not true.

The amount of energy we waste is SHOCKING!

8. ________ The number of machines and appliances we use has greatly increased in the last 100 years.
9. ________ Petroleum, oil, and hydropower are all fossil fuels.
10. ________ Burning coal causes acid rain.
11. ________ Our supply of fossil fuels is a renewable resource.
12. ________ Water, wind, and the sun are alternate sources of energy.
13. ________ Waste from nuclear power plants stays radioactive for thousands of years.
14. ________ Cars are one of the biggest producers of air pollution.

★ Think about the most interesting or important thing you have learned about energy and the way we use it. Write about it on the back of this sheet. ★

Name ________________________________

A POLLUTION WORD SEARCH

Circle each word you find in the word search. The words can be found either down or across.

DISPOSAL	AGENCY	PETROLEUM
AEROSOL	OZONE	INVERSION
GLOBAL	THERMAL	EXHAUST
CONTAMINATED	BATTERIES	SMOGGY

Name________________________________

POLLUTION HANDWRITING

sewage ________________________________

____

garbage ________________________________

____

solvents ________________________________

____

chemicals ________________________________

____

pesticides ________________________________

____

toxic ________________________________

____

fertilizers ________________________________

____

flammable ________________________________

____

hazardous ________________________________

____

corrosive ________________________________

____

Name ______________________________

WHAT IS POLLUTION?

As you read this story, circle the correct word in each numbered box at the bottome of this sheet.

Everything you do causes some pollution. Even breathing releases carbon dioxide into the air. Pollution is waste that is no longer useful to us. The 1.______________ environment can't take care of some wastes. When the environment can't take care of the waste, the 2.____________ changes. Usually the changes are not pleasant. Fish die. Air turns smoggy. Soil can no longer grow plants.

People have always 3.____________ the environment. Long ago there were 4.____________ people. Pollution was widely scattered and the natural environment 5.____________ absorb it. Pollution caused little 6.____________ in the environment. Since the industrial revolution in the 1700's and 1800's, pollution has been a bigger and bigger problem. More people and more machines meant more and 7.____________ pollution. By the 1950's every major city and waterway in North America were showing the effects of pollution. In the 1960's people became aware of this growing problem. Today many people are working hard to find out about 8.______________ and how to reduce it.

Everyone thinks we should fix pollution, but it is 9.____________ that simple. Pollution comes from the way we live. Most people like the way we live. They do not 10.__________ to give up things they enjoy. Factories that make the things we need and enjoy also make pollution. Cars take us where we want to go, but they also pollute. We enjoy listening to our portable radio, but the batteries often end up in landfills, polluting the soil and ground water. The pollution problem is very difficult, but people <u>can</u> change. We can choose to use our resources wisely and carefully. It's up to us!

1. waste natural carbon	2. environment pollution breathing	3. polluted planted useful	4. many pollution few	5. couldn't wouldn't could
6. change pollution natural	7. more less some	8. pollution growing nature	9. just more not	10. more make want

Name________________________________

WHAT A MESS!

As you read this story, circle the correct word in each numbered box at the bottome of this sheet.

Environmental pollution is one of our most serious problems. Polluted air 1.____________ many people to become sick. Pollution makes water 2.______________ to drink. Land that once produced food is now useless for farming because of pollution. There are many different kinds of pollution. Air, water, and soil can be contaminated by our 3.___________. We produce sewage and garbage. Solid wastes pile up in landfills. People cut down forests for wood, paper, and clearing for farm land. Domestic animals are allowed to overgraze and turn 4.________________ areas into deserts. We throw away valuable resources every day—aluminum cans, glass bottles, paper, etc. We even 5.__________ our indoor environment with solvents, cigarette smoke, and chemicals of all kinds.

Everything in the 6.____________ environment is connected to everything else. Pollution is one 7.________________ of the environmental that causes many changes throughout the entire environment. Burning coal causes air 8.______________. Rain mixes with the pollution and becomes acid rain. The acid 9.________________ falls on the land and damages soil and crops. In the rivers, streams, and 10.________________ acid rain kills fish. The original coal-smoke makes its way through the natural environment.

Just about everything we do produces waste of one kind or another. What we choose to do with these wastes is the important question. All of our activities will cause changes in our environment. We can continue to change it in ways that damage or we can choose to change our activities to improve the environment.

1.	2.	3.	4.	5.
brings can causes	good fresh unfit	damages environment activities	large small most	clean pollute value
6.	**7.**	**8.**	**9.**	**10.**
environment natural pollution	area activities useless	natural rain pollution	rain lake air	lands lakes air

Name ______________________________

WHAT'S IN THE AIR?

pollutants
vehicles
exhaust
respiratory
thermal
inversion
monitor
global
aerosol
ozone

1. Cars, trucks, and buses are different kinds of ______________.
2. A word that rhymes with "alone" is __________________.
3. Scientists _______________ or keep track of air quality.
4. Chemicals and smoke are _______________.
5. Spray cans are_____________________ cans.
6. The word __________________ has the same root word as "thermometer."

One of the major causes of pollution is the burning of fossil fuels. We burn fossil fuels to make electricity, heat homes, and power vehicles. When we burn fossil fuels, waste is released into the air. Walking along a busy street you can smell the exhaust of automobiles, trucks, and buses. Many homes have fireplaces or wood stoves. It is easy to see smoke rising from chimneys. Pollutants mix with the air we breathe. Air pollution can make people sick. People with respiratory diseases like asthma and bronchitis must stay indoors when air pollution is particularly bad.

Usually wind and weather scatter pollutants widely and help clear the air. Sometimes weather traps pollution near the ground. When a layer of warm air covers a pocket of cold air, it is called a thermal inversion. Such an inversion keeps the air moving or mixing. Pollutants stay near their source and build up. Air near large cities can become dangerously polluted. Scientists monitor air quality. Your local news programs probably give the current air quality reading as part of the daily weather report.

Name________________________________

WHAT'S IN THE AIR?, CONTINUED

Burning releases carbon dioxide into the air. Carbon dioxide is called the "greenhouse" gas. When you sit in a car with the windows rolled up on a sunny day you get very warm inside the car. The windows let heat in but don't let it out. Carbon dioxide in our atmosphere acts like window glass. The sun's heat passes through to the earth, but cannot go back out into space. This is called the "greenhouse effect." Because we are putting more and more carbon dioxide into the atmosphere, more heat is held in. Scientists call this "global warming." Since 1900 our average temperature has gone up almost 1 degree F. No one knows exactly what this change will mean. Many predict major weather changes and large scale flooding.

Chemicals that we use also damage the atmosphere. Chlorine in a chemical called CFC destroys ozone. CFC's are used in aerosol cans, air conditioners, and refrigerators. Ozone forms a protective layer about 30 miles above the earth. The ozone layer filters out the sun's harmful ultraviolet rays. These rays cause cancers and kill plants and animals. Scientists have found a hole in the ozone layer over Antarctica. Experts are concerned that this hole will grow as more ozone is destroyed. Nearly all countries have agreed to stop using CFC's to help save the earth's ozone layer.

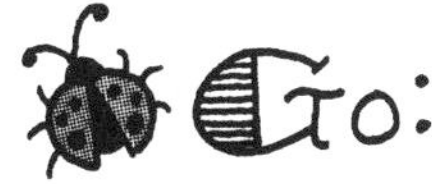

1. Carbon dioxide is called the ________________ "gas" because it holds heat in the atmosphere.

2. Air pollution does little harm to plants, animals, or people. (YES, NO)

3. Burning _________________ is a major cause of air pollution.

4. What does the ozone layer do for the earth? ____

   ____

5. A thermal (conversion, conversation, inversion) traps air pollution near the earth's surface.

6. What do scientists predict might happen as a result of global warming? ________________

   ____

   ____

Name ______________________________

WHAT'S IN THE WATER?

Ready:

pollutants dramatic petroleum eutrophication contaminated industries sewage pesticides chemicals hull

1. ____________________ is the only one-syllable word in the list.
2. ____________________ is a fossil fuel often called "oil."
3. Household waste mixed with used water is ________________.
4. ____________________ and ____________________ are used to improve crops.
5. Factories and mills that manufacture products are ____________________.
6. Something that happens quickly and causes people to notice might be described as ______________________.

Set:

Only about 1% of all the earth's water is available for us to use. We all need fresh water to live. You probably use about 100 gallons of water every day yourself! If we all need clean, fresh water, then why do we keep messing it up?

Water gets contaminated with waste from animals and humans. Some waste comes from industries like mills or factories. We dump our sewage into lakes, rivers, and oceans. We pour pesticides and chemicals on farm lands. Later, these pollutants are washed into our waterways.

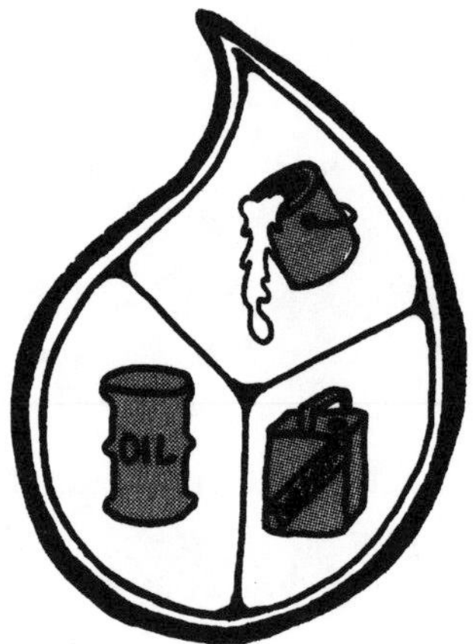

Pollutants make water unsafe for people to use. It also kills fish and other animals. Pollution upsets the natural balance of the water environment. Sometimes pollution makes water plants grow out of control. When the plants die and decay, most of the oxygen in the water is used up. Fish die from too little oxygen. This process is called eutrophication.

Thermal pollution has also become a problem for many industrialized countries. Many industries use water to cool things. When heated water is returned to the natural environment, it makes the waterway warmer. Temperature changes can damage plants and animals.

Name________________________________

WHAT'S IN THE WATER?, CONTINUED

Water pollution usually gets worse gradually. People don't always notice small changes. People do notice one type of water pollution, however. This pollution happens quickly and its effects are dramatic. This type of pollution is an oil spill.

We depend on fossil fuel like petroleum. Petroleum must be moved from where it is found to where it is needed. Huge ships called oil tankers move the oil. Sometimes these huge tankers have accidents and spill oil into the ocean. The oil can wash up on the beaches and cause even more damage.

In 1989, the Exxon Valdez, an oil tanker, ran aground in Prince William Sound. This area of Alaska was known for its unspoiled natural beauty. The broken hull of the Exxon Valdez spilled 11 million gallons of crude oil. Beaches were fouled more than 1000 miles away. Tens of thousands of sea birds, eagles, and sea otters died. No one knows what all of the long-term effects of this huge spill might be.

Water pollution is a serious problem in North America, China, Japan, Eastern Europe, and the former Soviet Union. Many countries have passed laws to protect their waterways. Laws limit how much and what type of things may be released into the water. Most cities in the United States treat sewage to make it safer to put into the water, but some large cities are still dumping raw sewage into rivers.

1. You use about (10, 100, 1000) gallons of fresh, clean water each day.

2. What are three pollutants we release into our waterways? ______________________________

   ____

3. Pollution upsets the natural balance of the water environment. (YES, NO)

4. When industries return heated water to rivers, lakes, or oceans, it can cause ________________ pollution.

5. __________________ spills can cause a huge amount of damage to the environment very quickly.

6. How have some countries tried to slow water pollution? ______________________________

   ____

   ____

Name ______________________________

THE TOXIC PYRAMID

There are many toxic or poisonous chemicals polluting our environment. Chemicals are used in fertilizers, pesticides, and nearly all industries. Some chemicals break down quickly in the environment. Some toxic pollutants stay in the environment for a long, long time. These decay very slowly and can cause much damage.

One pesticide that stays in the environment for a long time is DDT. The initials DDT stand for dichloro-diphenyl-trichloroethane. DDT is sprayed on crops to kill insects that are harmful to the crops. This seems like a good thing, but DDT creates many problems in the environment.

DDT is a fat-soluble chemical. This means that it stays in the body fat of animals. The chemical is sprayed on crops and rain washes it into streams. DDT is absorbed into <u>tiny water plants</u> and <u>animals</u>. Small fish feed on these tiny plants and animals. Bigger fish eat the <u>small fish</u>. Because one <u>big fish</u> eats many small fish, the big fish gets a lot more DDT. More DDT builds up in the big fish each time it eats a small fish. The DDT is stored in the body fat of the fish. An <u>eagle</u> eats many big fish. The eagle may have 1000 times as much DDT in its body as the plants at the bottom of the food chain.

The pesticide, DDT, was banned in the United States in 1972. Before the Environmental Protection Agency stopped the use of this harmful chemical, it was used for more than 30 years. DDT harmed many animals and birds. The DDT caused the eggs of many birds of prey to become thin and brittle. Owl, hawk, and eagle eggs broke before they could hatch. Because very few chicks were hatched, the populations of these birds dropped alarmingly. The American Bald Eagle became an endangered species. The Peregrine Falcon disappeared from the Eastern United States. Since the ban on DDT, many species have begun to recover. However, DDT is still being used in many countries. The use of DDT is still a worldwide problem.

Name___________________________________

THE TOXIC PYRAMID, CONTINUED

Use the information from the article "Toxic Pyramid" to help you answer these questions.

1. What are the benefits of using pesticides such as DDT? ______________________________

____

____

2. What are the dangers of using pesticides such as DDT? ______________________________

____

____

3. Why would an eagle have more DDT in its body than a small fish? ____________________

____

____

Use this space to draw a toxic pyramid. Show the food chain and the creatures that are affected by pesticides. Use the underlined words from the article to help you.

Name ________________________________

HOUSEHOLD HAZARDS

It's in your house! It's going down your drain! It's poured out in backyards everywhere! It's polluting your water! This probably sounds like an advertisement for a scary movie, but these things are happening every day—in your neighborhood! What is it? It is household hazardous waste—chemicals that your family uses every day. Are there hazardous chemicals at your house? Do you use batteries, glue, or cosmetics? All of these things become hazardous waste when we throw them away.

We use toxic chemicals for cleaning, medicines, automobile products, gardening, and hobbies. To find hazardous products look for these words on the labels: poison, corrosive, flammable, warning, caution.

Hazardous chemicals can be harmful in many ways. Poisonous products can make you sick if you swallow them. Corrosive products cause burns on skin or eyes. Flammable products are easily ignited and may produce vapors that can explode. If hazardous waste is disposed of improperly, it pollutes our environment. These harmful chemicals end up in the air we breathe, the water we drink, and the food we eat.

Most people have hazardous waste in their homes. Many people dispose of these wastes improperly because they don't think about how harmful the products are. You may not think that a small amount will hurt. Every day millions of people dump small amounts of household chemicals. That adds up to a big problem.

You can be part of the hazardous waste solution. Use the least toxic product that will do the job. Choose rechargeable batteries. Try a homemade window cleaner. Two tablespoons of vinegar in one quart of warm water will do a good job. Buy only what you need and use it up. If you need only a small amount of paint, choose the smallest container. If you don't use all of it, give the remaining paint to someone who will use it. Always follow the label directions carefully. The label will tell you how to use and dispose of a hazardous product safely.

Name________________________________

HOUSEHOLD HAZARDS, CONTINUED

Use the article "Household Hazards" to help you answer these questions.

1. What are five hazardous household products? __________

____

____

2. What words on the labels of products tell you that they may be toxic? ______________

____

3. Tell three ways that hazardous household chemicals are harmful. ______________

____

____

____

4. Why do many people improperly dispose of household hazardous waste? ____________

____

____

____

5. What are some ways you can be part of the household hazardous waste solution? ______

____

____

____

On the back of this sheet list as many household hazardous wastes as you can. You may want to do a "hazardous product search" in your home. Compare your list with other students and add products if you wish. Your teacher may want to complete a class list. Try to find safer alternatives to some of these products.

Name ______________________________

HAZARDOUS RESEARCH

Keeping hazardous waste out of our environment is everyone's responsibility. Sometimes people dump harmful products simply because they don't know what should be done with them. You can find out how to safely dispose of many household hazardous wastes.

Nearly all hazardous products have warning labels. These labels clearly state how to dispose of the products. If the label doesn't give enough information, there are other ways to find out what to do. You can write or phone the product's manufacturer. The address or phone number should be on the label. You can contact a government agency such as the Environmental Protection Agency or the Food and Drug Administration. These agencies are listed under U.S. Government in your phone book. You can get information from your local waste collection company, department of health, or public library. Find out how you can be part of the household hazardous waste solution.

Use any or all of the resources listed above to find out how to safely dispose of each of these hazardous household products. You may ask for help from your parents or other adults. The more people who know about these solutions—the better!

OVEN CLEANER ______________________________

____

____

USED ANTIFREEZE ______________________________

____

____

Name ____________________

HAZARDOUS RESEARCH, CONTINUED

Share what you find out about toxic products. Spread the word.

SPRAY CAN OF PESTICIDES ____________________

____

____

____

OIL-BASED PAINT ____________________

____

____

BATTERIES ____________________

____

____

MEDICINES ____________________

____

____

KEROSENE ____________________

____

____

USED MOTOR OIL ____________________

____

____

WATER-BASED PAINT ____________________

____

____

Name ______________________________

SUPPLIES SURPRISE

You probably don't know how many different things you use each week in your own classroom. You can monitor your supplies to see how your activities are affecting the earth. You can make your classroom more earth friendly. Maybe you can even influence other classes in your school to join you in pollution solutions.

Work with at least three other people to gather information. The members of your group should decide how to divide the work. You may have to ask questions of the adults who work at your school. You may need to save, count, weigh, or measure items. Use your imagination. Work together. Find out!

Look at the activities you do each day for one week. On the back of this sheet, list all the supplies you use. Include chalk, glue, crayons, pens, batteries, paper cups, plastic bags, etc. Share the list in your group each day. Add items to your list if you wish. Try to estimate how much of each type of supply your class is using. Note the estimated amount on your list.

At the end of the week, discuss these questions with your group. Record your ideas.

1. How many different kinds of supplies did your class use this week? ____________________

____

____

____

2. What five items were used the most during the week? ______________________________

____

____

____

Name________________________

SUPPLIES SURPRISE, CONTINUED

3. What supplies were used the most carefully and wisely? ______________

4. What supplies were wasted or not used fully? ______________

Some art supplies contain toxic chemicals like ethanol.

5. What supplies came from nonrenewable resources like petroleum and plastic? ______________

6. What items came from recycled or reused materials? ______________

7. How were supplies disposed of in your classroom this week? ______________

Decide on three things you and your classmates could do to use and dispose of supplies more wisely. They are POLLUTION SOLUTIONS! On the back of this paper, make a poster about one of your ideas. Display the posters where other classes can see them and learn from you.

Name ______________________________

NOISE, NOISE, NOISE!

Noise is one type of pollution that many people just don't think about. Noise pollution is a problem for many people, especially those living in large cities. Loud noises can be annoying, but they can also damage people's hearing. People living and working around loud noises can gradually lose their ability to hear.

Sound is measured in decibels. A whisper is about 20 decibels. The sound of a jet plane taking off is about 140 decibels. A rock band puts out about 120 decibels of noise. Anything over 100 decibels can cause hearing damage. Noises between 60 and 100 decibels are considered annoying by most people.

Quiet, please.

Use one of these words on each numbered line to complete the graph: vacuum cleaner, jet plane, rock band, whisper, talking.

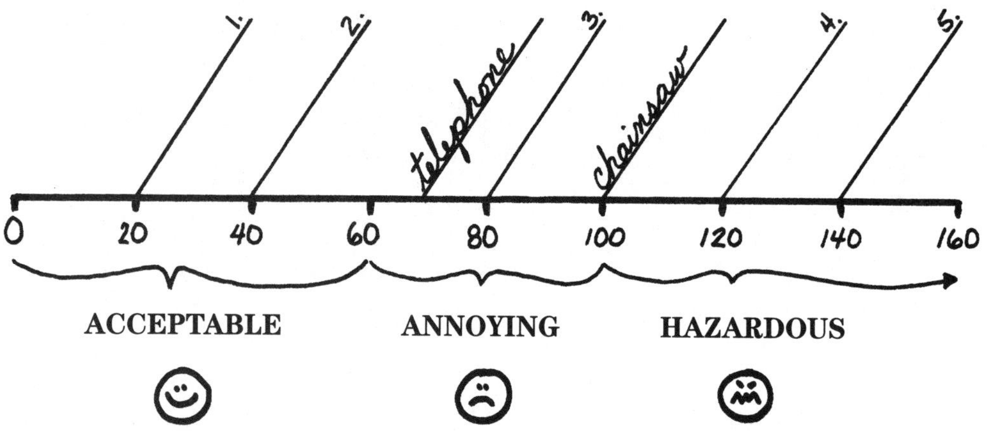

6. Which sounds could cause hearing damage? ______________________________

____

7. Which sounds are generally considered annoying? ______________________________

____

8. How could you protect yourself against noise pollution? ______________________________

____

____

____

Name___________________________

BEACH PICKUP

More than one million sea birds and marine mammals die each year from our carelessness. These creatures die when they become tangled in litter we leave behind. They die by strangling on trash that floats in our waterways or washes up on our beaches. Circle the things in this picture that don't belong in our natural environment.

Name ______________________________

POLLUTION PROBLEMS

Add, subtract, mulitiply, or divide to find out more about pollution. Share these facts with your family and friends.

WORK SPACE

1. Each gallon of gas used by a car releases 19 pounds of carbon dioxide into the air. The average car's tank holds 15 gallons of gas. How much carbon dioxide is produced by each tank of gas?

   ____

2. Many animals die from strangling on plastic. Each year plastic litter kills 1,000,000 sea birds, 50,000 seals, and 100,000 other marine animals. How many animals altogether die each year from plastic?

   ____

3. Using recycled paper for printing one week's Sunday edition of The New York Times would save 75,000 trees. How many trees could be saved in one year?

   ____

4. There have been 35,000 pesticides introduced since 1945. Only 3500 of these chemicals have been tested to see if they are harmful to people. How many pesticides have never been tested for safety?

   ____

5. A typical American family of four uses about 400 gallons of water each day. How much water does one person use each day?____________ How much water does one person use in a year?

   ____

Name___________________________________

POLLUTION QUICK CHECK

Use the word box to help you complete the sentences.

pesticides	ozone	environment	greenhouse	oxygen
wastes	pollution	acid rain	ecology	hazardous

1. __________________ is waste that is no longer useful to us.
2. Burning fossil fuels causes air pollution and __________________.
3. Chlorine in CFC's destroys the earth's __________________ layer.
4. Carbon dioxide is called the __________________ gas.
5. Water gets contaminated with animal and human __________________.
6. __________________ sprayed on crops can pollute nearby streams.
7. Used batteries are a __________________ household waste product.

Write "YES" for true and "NO" for not true.

8. ________ People have always polluted the natural environment.
9. ________ Acid rain is the main cause of global warming and the greenhouse effect.
10. ________ Sometimes pollution upsets the natural balance and water plants grow out of control.
11. ________ Thermal pollution happens when warm air is trapped near the ground.
12. ________ Few laws exist to protect our environment from pollution.
13. ________ Animals at the top of the food chain can build up large amounts of chemicals in their bodies.
14. ________ Small amounts of toxic wastes may be poured down the drain safely.

★★ Think about the most interesting or important thing you have learned about environmental pollution. Write about it on the back of this sheet.

Name ______________________________

Circle each of the words you find in the word search. The words can be found either down or across.

A	I	C	M	P	E	O	F	R	S	C	B	O	P	S	U	T
J	B	L	D	C	O	N	S	E	R	V	A	T	I	O	N	W
H	K	P	N	O	Q	G	Y	A	B	D	N	Q	R	X	V	Z
S	T	O	R	M	D	R	A	I	N	S	N	E	Y	C	A	G
A	V	L	T	P	X	E	Z	J	L	I	E	B	D	F	R	W
N	U	L	W	O	G	S	H	K	H	J	D	Q	U	R	V	S
I	E	U	F	S	I	P	P	M	Z	S	A	X	T	U	E	C
T	K	T	L	T	R	O	N	O	D	O	Y	J	D	N	B	H
A	M	I	N	L	A	N	D	F	I	L	L	F	I	O	G	K
R	J	O	B	K	D	S	H	F	S	I	J	M	C	F	H	A
Y	A	N	I	C	G	I	E	I	P	D	L	E	N	F	B	D
Q	B	R	O	K	P	B	H	T	O	W	J	X	E	Z	B	C
A	D	U	R	A	B	L	E	U	S	A	W	F	Y	G	D	A
L	I	F	C	S	M	E	V	I	A	S	Z	I	S	K	U	M
A	H	D	C	K	P	N	F	Q	L	T	H	T	J	B	L	W
G	E	B	J	D	E	O	N	G	R	E	A	Y	D	V	X	C

POLLUTION
SANITARY
LANDFILL
SOLID WASTE

RESPONSIBLE
BANNED
DURABLE
DISPOSAL

CONSERVATION
COMPOST
STORM DRAIN
RUNOFF

Name________________________________

CONSERVATION HANDWRITING

Nearly half of American consumers regularly recycle cans and bottles.

reduce ________________________________

____

reuse ________________________________

____

recycle ________________________________

____

technology ________________________________

____

economic ________________________________

____

disposable ________________________________

____

leach ________________________________

____

contaminate ________________________________

____

incinerator ________________________________

____

compost ________________________________

____

Name ______________________________

WHY DO WE POLLUTE?

As you read this story, circle the correct word in each numbered box at the bottom of this sheet.

Nearly everyone would agree that pollution is a bad thing. Many types of pollution could be 1.______________ reduced. Then why do we keep right on polluting our environment? Why don't we just clean it up?

There are several 2.______________ why we continue to dump pollution into our 3.______________. One reason is our dependence on technology. Fertilizer and 4.______________ make a wide variety of appealing foods readily available at reasonable prices. Cars take us where we want to go whenever we like. Factories produce an incredible 5.________ of products from running shoes to computers. All of these activities pollute our environment.

Many ways of preventing pollution are expensive. We have many ways to reuse 6.______________ products from industry. There are also ways to clean 7.____________ from many waste products. Both of these cost more money than simply dumping the pollutants. Acid rain is an example of pollution that happens for economic reasons. Scientists have developed ways of cleaning 8.__________ from coal-smoke, but the processes are very expensive. People don't want to pay twice as much for electricity in order to have cleaner power-generating plants.

People enjoy convenience. We are in the habit of 9._________ away and creating waste. Is your lunch packaged in material that is thrown away? Do you use a paper bag, plastic wrap, or foil? Durable products that are washed and 10.______________ save the environment, but disposable packaging is handy. Cars are another example of convenience pollution. A bus or train may take longer or make us plan to leave earlier, but they save fuel and pollute much less.

We continue to pollute because we depend on technology. We don't want to pay to clean up after ourselves. Protecting the environment takes time and thought.

1. most any greatly	2. pollutes numbers reasons	3. environment industries community	4. pesticides pollution agricultural	5. size appealing number
6. many waste pollute	7. prices pollutants environment	8. sulfer water industry	9. recycling throwing disposable	10. durable packing reused

Name ___________________________

RACHEL CARSON

As you read this story, circle the correct word in each numbered box at the bottom of this sheet.

On May 27, 1907 Rachel Carson was born in Pennsylvania. As a child, Rachel loved books and music. When she was just eight 1.__________ old, Rachel began creating books of her own. No one 2.__________ she would, one day, write a book that would change the way people 3.__________ at the world.

Rachel Carson wanted to be a writer. In college she discovered a love for science. She was particularly interested in the oceans and 4.__________ life. Rachel appreciated the interdependence of all living creatures. She wrote beautiful books about life in the sea. Many people enjoyed her 5.__________ and learned to share her love of nature.

In the 1950's DDT was being 6.__________ a miracle. This deadly pesticide was sprayed to kill insects that ruined crops. More food could be grown cheaply. Rachel Carson didn't 7.__________ DDT was a miracle. She believed it was poisoning the whole environment along with the bugs. Huge numbers of birds were dying 8.__________ areas that were sprayed.

Rachel Carson decided that she had to do something about the use of DDT. She had to let people know the 9.__________ of this powerful chemical. Rachel used her talent and experience to write a book, Silent Spring. The book was released in 1962 and many people attacked Rachel's work. Many scientists believed anything they invented, including DDT, was good. They 10.__________ want to listen to what Rachel had to say. But Rachel had written the truth. Within ten years DDT was banned in the United States and people were thinking about the effects of other chemicals.

Rachel Carson started something important. She used her talent to make people listen to what they didn't want to hear. One person can make a difference!

Rachel Carson studied the sea for years before she ever saw the ocean.

1.	2.	3.	4.	5.
months days years	had liked knew	looked wanted books	sea science music	books writer living
6. called used creatures	7. want think make	8. away near large	9. dangers names birds	10. wanted always didn't

Name ________________________________

DOWN IN THE DUMPS

Ready:

sanitary leach solid foul groundwater landfill wastes contaminate reserve dispose

1. Landfill and ______________ are both compound words.
2. Something that is not gas or liquid is ______________.
3. The amount of something that we have left for our use is our ________________.
4. ________________ rhymes with the word "beach."
5. The word "fowl" is the homonym of ________________.
6. ________________ are all of the things that are no longer useful to us that we throw away.

Every day we throw things away. We toss cans, bottles, boxes, and bags. Into the trash can they go along with food scraps, yard wastes, broken furniture, and all sorts of things we simply don't want anymore. Where does all this stuff go?

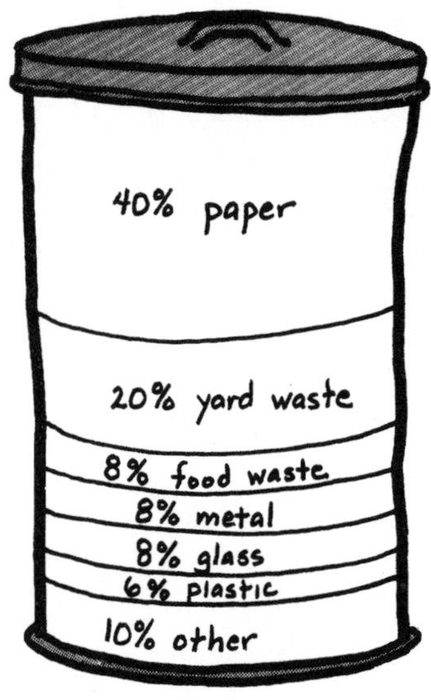

Not long ago most garbage was disposed of in much the same way the ancient Greeks disposed of their garbage. It was dumped. An open field or pit was used to simply pile up the garbage. This system had some big problems. Garbage dumps are ugly, smelly, and attract flies and rats. Many dumps also burned garbage, causing air pollution. Unfortunately, some communities still use garbage dumps to dispose of their solid wastes.

In 1976 a law was passed in the United States to protect the environment. The Resource Conservation and Recovery Act set new stricter standards for disposal of solid wastes. Communities found new ways to deal with garbage. Sanitary landfills began to replace city dumps. In a landfill layers of garbage are covered by layers of soil. This solved the problems of ugly garbage blowing in the wind and smelling foul. Rats and insects are also kept out by the dirt layers. However, sanitary landfills have some of the same problems as an open dump. Pollutants in garbage get into the soil and leach into the groundwater. The water becomes unsafe to drink.

Name ______________________________

DOWN IN THE DUMPS, CONTINUED

Another way that communities dispose of garbage is incineration. Incinerators burn the solid waste at very high temperatures. The leftover ash is sent to a landfill. The heat produced by the burning can be used to heat homes or to generate electricity. Incinerators pollute the air. Ash from incinerators often contain dangerous chemicals and heavy metals. These can contaminate the groundwater around the landfills.

Resource recovery is another plan often used with incinerators. Garbage is sorted to collect out valuable resources such as aluminum, tin, and glass. This greatly reduces the amount of garbage that must be burned or buried. It also saves limited resources and energy reserves. In some communities resource recovery begins in individual homes and businesses. These people sort their trash and collect recyclable materials right in their homes or businesses. The materials are picked up separately from other trash and sold for reuse by indus try.

Many people believe we must learn to throw away less and use our resources more wisely. We each need to take responsibility for the messes we make and the garbage we generate.

We make enough trash in the U.S. each day to fill the New Orleans Superdome— twice!

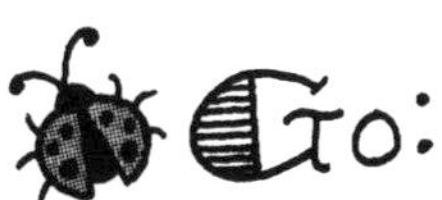

1. Some communities still use open dumps to dispose of their solid wastes. (YES, NO)

2. Pollutants in landfills can leach into the soil and ______________ the groundwater.

3. In ____________ ______________ layers of dirt cover layers of garbage.

4. Incinerating garbage causes (air, water, soil) pollution.

5. What happens at a resource recovery center? ______________________________

____

6. Where is ash from most incinerators disposed of? ______________________

Name ______________________________

THE THREE R'S

- landfill
- incinerator
- over-package
- durable
- researchers
- collections
- container
- charity
- recycle
- aluminum

1. A high temperature furnace for burning garbage is an ______________________________.
2. Many manufacturers ________________ products to make them more attractive to buyers.
3. An item that will last a long time is called ________________.
4. Some ________________ organizations collect used clothing and furniture for reuse.
5. ____________________ is a metal commonly used for making soft drink cans.
6. ____________________ are scientists who study a problem to look for solutions.

Very few things that end up in landfills and incinerators need to be there. Most of our garbage is actually full of valuable resources. If we all practiced the three R's there would be far less trash to deal with. We would be protecting our air, water, and soil from pollution. What are the three R's?—Reduce, Reuse, and Recycle.

The first of the three R's is reduce. We can reduce the amount of garbage and pollution we cause. Many items we buy are over-packaged. A small toy is glued to a cardboard display and sealed under a plastic bubble. All of the package becomes garbage for one small item. Buy products in large sizes. One large box of breakfast cereal requires less packaging than two small boxes. Don't buy things you don't really need. Many things we buy are quickly forgotten and thrown away. Try trading games, tapes, or CD's with your friends instead of buying new ones. Rent or borrow things you only need for a short time. When you buy clothes, choose durable things that you will like and wear for a long time. If you reduce, you will save the environment and your money, too.

Name________________________________

THE THREE R'S, CONTINUED

The second R is reuse. Don't be too quick to throw things away. Find new ways to use old things. Plastic food containers can hold art supplies or your collections. Greeting card fronts can become bookmarks or post cards. Old clothing can be repaired, cleaned, and donated to charity. Scrap paper can be cut and stapled into scratch pads. If you use your imagination you can surely think of many ways to reuse the things we throw away each day.

The last of the three R's is recycle. Every year Americans toss away 40 million soft drink cans and bottles. If all of these containers were placed end to end they would reach to the moon—and back—20 times! Aluminum, glass, tin, paper, and some plastics can be recycled. In recycling, used materials are collected and used to make new products. Researchers are finding new ways to use recycled materials, but the most important part of recycling is you. People must change the way they think about trash and learn to recycle. Some communities have curbside recycling. People put out bins of sorted recyclables along with their trash. In other places, recyclables must be taken to drop-off centers. Does your community have a recycling plan?

If we all try to use the three R's we can protect our environment. Pick one idea from each of the three R's and start today.

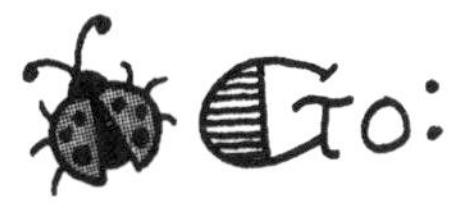

More than 80% of all the stuff we throw away could be recycled.

1. Where does most of our garbage end up? ______________

2. More than (30%, 50%, 80%) of our garbage could be recycled and made into new, useful products.

3. What are the three R's? ______________, ______________ and ______________

4. What is over-packaging? ____

____

5. Aluminum, glass, and tin are all materials that can be ______________________.

6. Tell one thing you can do to use the three R's to protect your environment. ________

____

Name ________________________________

WHY RECYCLE?

BECAUSE YOU CARE!

More than 80% of the stuff we throw in the trash is recyclable. That means that we are wasting huge amounts of valuable resources. By recycling you can save these resources and make your community a cleaner and healthier place for everyone.

BECAUSE YOU ARE SMART!

Recycling doesn't cost any money. It saves you money because you have less trash to dispose of. You can make the water and air cleaner and reduce pollution in your community. You can be part of the pollution solution.

BECAUSE IT IS EASY!

Recycling takes a small amount of time and some planning. You can start with something simple like newspaper or aluminum cans. In most communities you can recycle glass, metal, cardboard, motor oil, batteries, yard waste, and plastics. Once you start, recycling will become a habit. You will probably be looking for other ways to use the 3 R's.

Why is recycling a good idea? ________________________________

____

____

____

____

____

____

____

____

Name ____________________

WHY RECYCLE?, CONTINUED

Draw or list some of the things that could be put into each recycling bin below.

★PAPER★

★GLASS★

★METAL★

★OTHER★

Name ______________________________

A DRAINING EXPERIENCE

When rain falls on a forest, the water is absorbed by the trees, plants, and soil. When rains falls on a roof or parking lot, the water is not absorbed. The rain runs off these hard surfaces. Where does all that water go?

Look at the street near your home or school. Near the curb you might see a grate. That grate covers a storm drain. Storm drains are like a separate sewer system for runoff. Runoff is all the water that flows off of streets, roofs, and parking lots when it rains.

Storm drains keep streets from flooding and becoming impassable. Drains also protect against erosion by the running water.

Storm drains flow directly into the natural waterways. The water collected by storm drains is returned to streams, rivers, and lakes. Usually this water is not treated the way household and industrial wastes are treated. This can be a big problem. Many people get rid of hazardous wastes by dumping them down a storm drain. These wastes contaminate our waterways. Paint, antifreeze, and motor oil do <u>not</u> belong in a storm drain!

If more people knew the dangers of dumping wastes into storm drains, our waterways would be much cleaner and safer. Young people in many communities are spreading the word. Clubs, groups, and classes are stenciling warnings on storm drain grates. The warnings remind people not to put wastes into the storm drain grates. In many areas the local public works department will help with paint and even stencils. Maybe your class, scout group, or neighborhood could do a project like this in your community.

 Use the article to help you answer these questions.

1. What is a storm drain? ______________________________

____

____

Name________________________________

A DRAINING EXPERIENCE, CONTINUED

2. What are the benefits of having a storm drain system? ________________________________

3. Where does storm drain water go? ________________________________

4. What is the problem with people and storm drains? ________________________________

5. What is being done to solve the problems people create with storm drains? ____________

6. What could you do to get the word out in your community? ________________________

Think about how much runoff is caused by paved areas. On th back of this sheet, tell how you think we could reduce the runoff and need for storm drains.

Name ________________________________

AN ENVIRONMENTAL ISSUE

Many people are working on solutions to our environmental problems. The more you know about environmental issues, the better choices you can make in your own life. You can be a part of the solution. Maybe you will come up with important new answers. Spread the word! Share what you know with your friends and family.

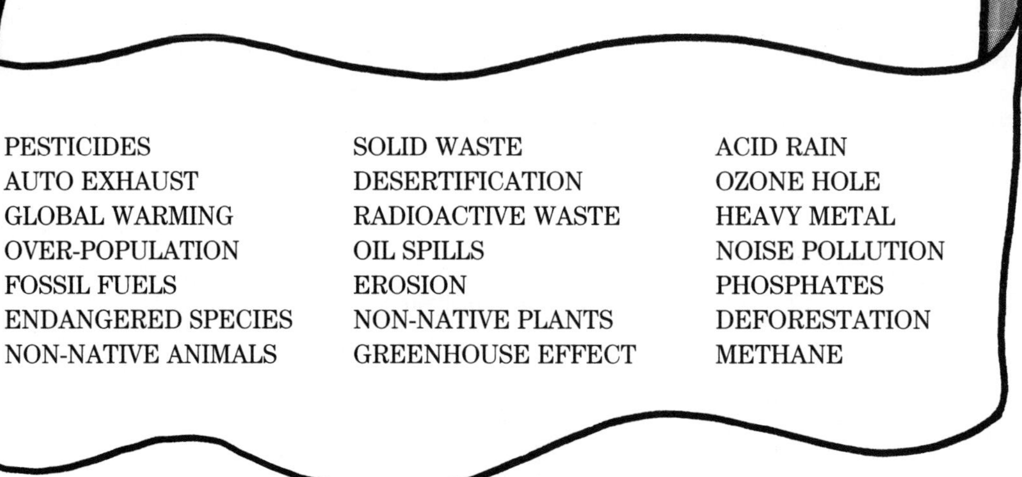

Choose three environmental issues you would like to know more about from the list above. Write the three issues in the spaces below.

1. ____
2. ____
3. ____

Use the index volume of an encyclopedia to help you find information about each issue.

Use other resources, too, if you like. Take notes on each issue on a separate sheet of paper. Find out what problems are part of each issue, where these problems exist, and what is being done about them. Note any interesting facts about your environmental issue. Complete "An Environmental Issue" sheet for <u>one</u> issue you researched.

AN ENVIRONMENTAL ISSUE, CONTINUED

____
(issue)

by______________________________
(your name)

How does your issue affect the environment? ______________________________

____

____

Why hasn't something been done to stop these effects? ______________________________

____

____

What is being done now and what needs to be done in the future to stop the harmful effects of this environmental issue? ______________________________

____

____

What is the most interesting thing you found out in doing your research on this issue?

____

____

____

____

THE ABC'S GO GREEN

Name ______________________________

Try to remember all the things you have learned about the environment. Work with a friend. Together, write an environmental fact or rule for each letter. A few are done for you.

A. *Automobiles release carbon dioxide into the air.*

B. ______________________________

C. ______________________________

D. ______________________________

E. ______________________________

F. ______________________________

G. ______________________________

H. ______________________________

I. ______________________________

J. ______________________________

K. ______________________________

L. ______________________________

Name______________________

THE ABC'S GO GREEN, CONTINUED

M. ______________________________

____

N. ______________________________

____

O. *One person can make a difference to our environment.*

____

P. ______________________________

____

Q. ______________________________

____

R. ______________________________

____

S. ______________________________

____

T. ______________________________

____

U. ______________________________

____

V. ______________________________

____

W. ______________________________

____

X. *Toxic wastes don't belong in your drain.*

____

Y. ______________________________

____

Z. ______________________________

____

Name ______________________________

WHAT'S COMPOST?

Nearly one third of the stuff that goes into our garbage is food scraps and yard waste. These wastes can be turned into a treasure called humus. Humus is a nutrient-rich mixture of decayed materials. When added to topsoil, humus also acts like a sponge to hold water and keep the soil from washing away when it rains.

How do we get this treasure from our food and yard wastes? Waste can be turned into humus by composting. Composting speeds up the natural decaying process by "cooking" wastes in a compost pile. A compost pile is made of layers. Green vegetation, like grass clippings, puts nitrogen in the compost. Dry layers, like chipped twigs or dry leaves, add bulk. Garden soil or manure adds necessary bacteria.

Once you have a compost pile, you can make it work faster by turning or mixing the layers every week. When you turn your compost, you may see steam rising from the center of the pile. Decay produces heat. In a few weeks your compost will be ready to add to your garden. You've made treasure from trash!

Write "YES" for each statement that is true. Write "NO" for each statement that is not true.

1. _________ More than half of the stuff we throw away is food and yard waste.

2. _________ Humus is a natural fertilizer made of decayed materials.

3. _________ Food scraps and yard wastes can be turned into topsoil by composting.

4. _________ Compost is cooked in layers and stirred in a huge pot.

5. _________ Compost piles have layers of green clippings, dry bulk, and soil.

6. _________ Your compost will decay faster if you turn or mix it once a week.

On the back of this sheet, rewrite each false statement and make it true.

Name ______________________________

A CONSERVATION PUZZLE

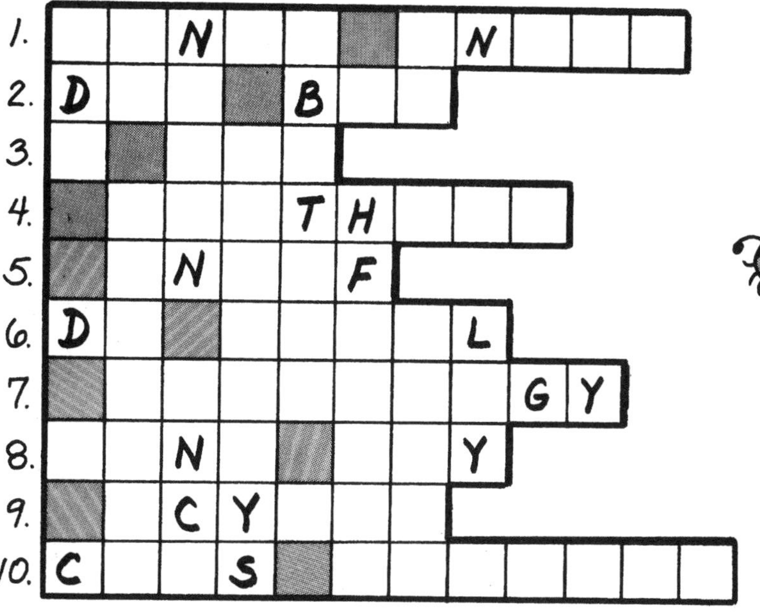

Use the clues to help you complete the puzzle. Unscramble the letters in the shaded boxes to solve the riddle.

CLUES

1. Pesticides and chemicals can leach into the ground and ___________ groundwater.
2. Choosing ___________ goods and products protects our environment.
3. Solid __________ is all of the stuff we throw away because we no longer have a use for them.
4. Making wise choices saves money and keeps our earth cleaner and ____________.
5. Rain water that pours from roofs, streets, and parking lots is _____________.
6. Improper __________ of hazardous wastes can cause big problems.
7. Economics, convenience, and advances in ____________ are causes of pollution.
8. Most of our garbage ends up in incinerators and ___________ landfills.
9. Reduce, Reuse, and __________ are the three R's of solid waste disposal.
10. Making choices to use our natural resources wisely is ______________.

What have you become ?!

Name ______________________________

A LITTLE LOGIC

Five children decide to start recycling. Each child chooses something different to recycle. No two children recycle the same thing. The children's names are Jamal, Barbara, Kate, Mike, and Maria. The things they decide to recycle are glass, newspaper, aluminum, tin cans, and mixed paper.

Use the clues to help you fill in the matrix and find out who recycled each of the items.

CLUES:

A. Jamal doesn't recycle bottles.

B. Barbara doesn't recycle junk mail and neither does Jamal.

C. Kate doesn't recycle the Sunday paper.

D. Jamal doesn't recycle soft drink containers.

E. Maria and Jamal don't do anything with paper.

F. Maria recycles foil and soda cans.

G. Kate recycles bottles and jars.

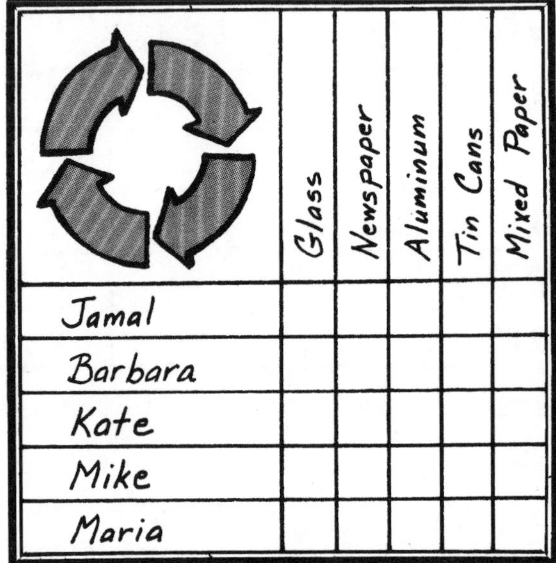

	Glass	Newspaper	Aluminum	Tin Cans	Mixed Paper
Jamal					
Barbara					
Kate					
Mike					
Maria					

WHO RECYCLES...

GLASS? ______________________________

NEWSPAPER? ______________________________

ALUMINUM? ______________________________

TIN CANS? ______________________________

MIXED PAPER? ______________________________

The energy saved by recycling one glass bottle will light a light bulb for four hours.

Name________________________________

CONSERVATION QUICK CHECK

Use the word box to help you complete the sentences.

compost	technology	pesticides	responsibility		
recycle	resources	runoff	incinerator	industrial	landfills

1. We can ______________ glass, aluminum, paper, and some plastics.
2. If we make better choices about waste disposal, we save valuable ______________.
3. One reason for pollution is our dependence on advances in ________________.
4. ____________________ is rain water pouring from hard surfaces like streets and roofs.
5. ____________________ and fertilizers can enter ground water and cause damage to plants and animals.
6. City dumps have been largely replaced by sanitary ______________.
7. We all must take _________________ for the environmental messes we make.

Write "YES" for true and "NO" for not true.

Make a difference... Be EARTH SMART!

8. ________ Almost all human activities cause some pollution to the environment.
9. ________ Rachel Carson was a scientist and writer who told the world about the harmful effects of pesticides.
10. ________ Incinerators are clean, efficient ways to dispose of solid wastes.
11. ________ We can recycle everything we use so we will have no pollution.
12. ________ Giving things we no longer need to someone who can use them is a good way to reduce waste.
13. ________ Storm drains are a good place to dispose of oil and antifreeze.
14. ________ Few people are working on solutions to our environmental problems.

★ Think about the most interesting or important thing you have learned about solid waste, recycling, and resource conservation. Write about it on the back of this sheet.

Conservation Notes

Name ______________________________

SECTION FIVE

ANSWER KEY

SECTION TWO: ENVIRONMENT

A LAND WORD SEARCH • page 24

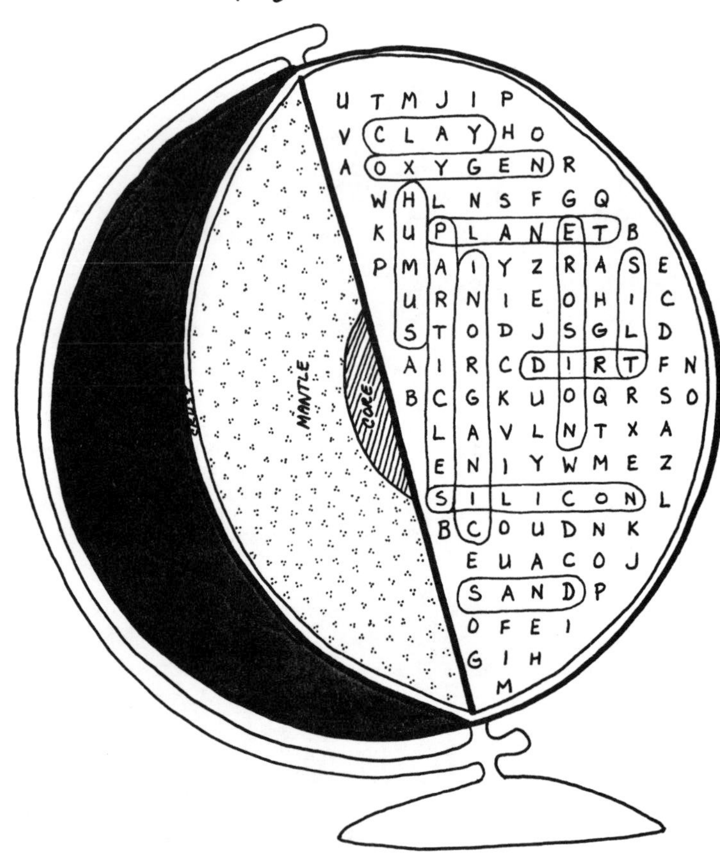

WHAT'S SO SPECIAL ABOUT EARTH? • page 26

1. system
2. star
3. planet
4. animals
5. support
6. temperatures
7. would
8. survive
9. water
10. right

IS DIRT IMPORTANT? • page 27

1. living
6. rocks

2. eat
3. layer
4. rocks
5. break
7. long
8. soil
9. animal
10. soil

THE CHANGING EARTH • page 30-31

Ready:

1. molten
2. dissolves
3. redepositing
4. Evaporation
5. Earthquakes
6. magma

Go:

1. slowly
2. earthquakes; volcanic eruptions
3. True
4. Wind, water, temperature
5. Minerals
6. soil
7. Freezing water expands and breaks up rocks.

ROCKY ROAD • page 32-33

Ready:

1. sedimentary
2. Oxygen
3. inorganic, igneous
4. continuously
5. metamorphic

Go:

1. inorganic
2. 98%
3. three
4. igneous
5. sedimentary
6. metamorphic
7. false
8. minerals

MORE THAN JUST DIRT • *page 34-35*

1. sand
2. silt
3. clay
4. silt
5. clay
6. sand
7. clay
8. sand
9. clay
10. silt
11. silt
12. sand
13. sand
14. clay

ONE CONTINENT? • *page 41*

1. Megener
2. continents
3. plate
4. Atlantic
5. ocean
6. evidence
7. Africa

COORDINATE THE COORDINATES • *page 42*

LAND QUICK CHECK • *page 43*

1. planet
2. magma
3. metamorphic, igneous, sedimentary
4. finite
5. renewable
6. environment
7. erosion
8. NO
9. NO
10. NO
11. YES
12. NO
13. NO
14. YES

A WATER WORD SEARCH • *page 44*

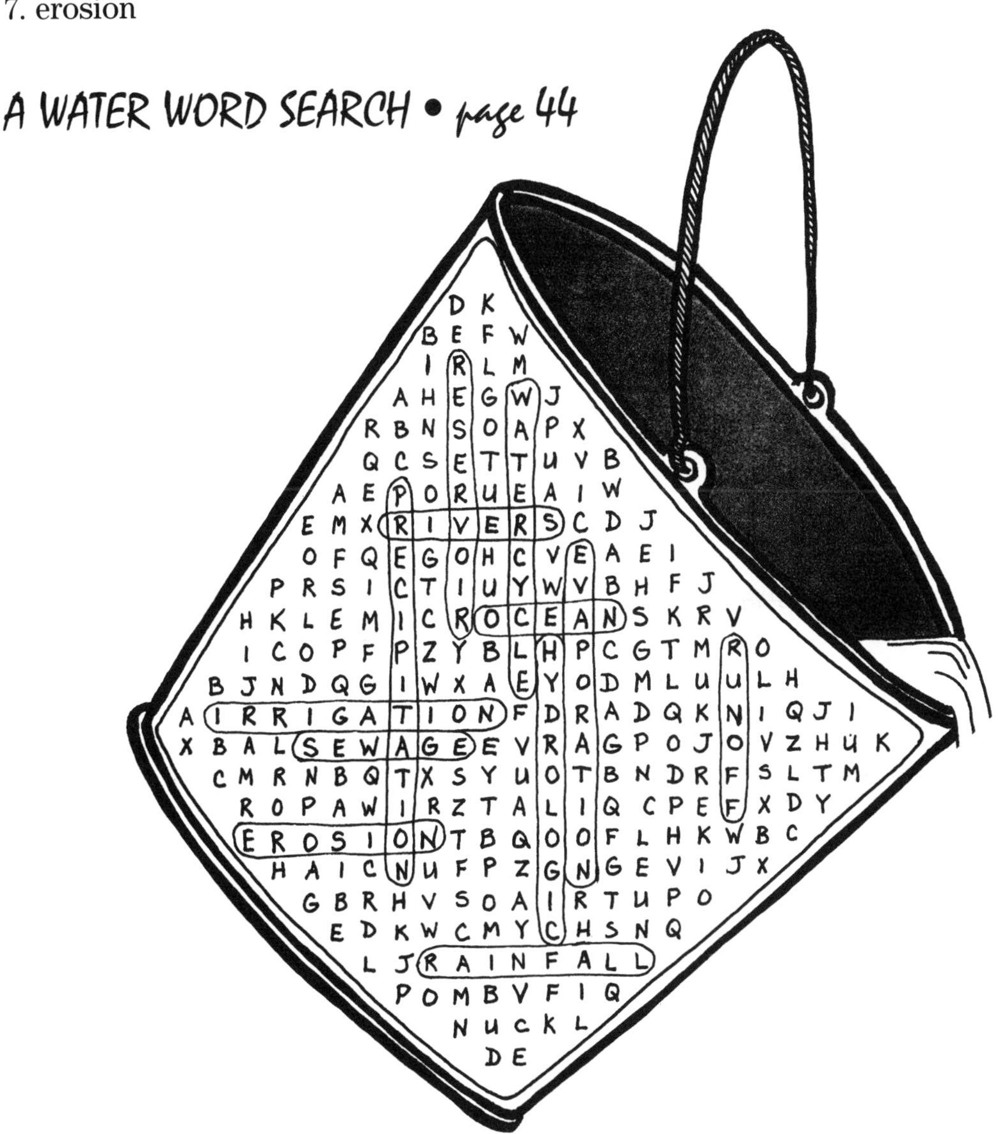

WHERE IS ALL THE WATER? • page 46

1. planet
2. water
3. person
4. lifeless
5. years
6. used
7. covers
8. Salty
9. water
10. many

FOOD FROM THE SEA • page 47

1. people
2. catch
3. them
4. tasty
5. important
6. harvests
7. fish
8. cured
9. sea
10. Quotas

THE WATER CYCLE • page 48-49

1–4. Answers will vary.
5. NO
6. YES
7. NO
8. YES
9. YES
10. YES

HOW WE USE WATER • page 50-51

1. YES
2. YES
3. YES
4. NO
5. YES
6. material
7. irrigate
8. homes
9. billion
10. electricity

TURN ON THE WATER • *page* 52-53

Ready:

1. flocs
2. reservoir
3. coagulation, filtration, disinfection
4. impurities
5. purify
6. alum

Go:

1. surface;ground
2. No
3. Chlorine
4. water table
5. pushes water through pipes
6. dirt

DOWN THE DRAIN • *page* 54-55

Ready:

1. waste water
2. Contaminates
3. conveniences
4. Sludge
5. tertiary
6. Effluent

Go:

1. YES
2. *Any three of the following:* food particles, bodywaste, soap, dirt, bacteria, chemicals
3. 99%
4. to kill harmful bacteria
5. sludge
6. grease/oil

SOLAR PURIFIER • *page* 60

2 - 4 - 1 - 6 - 5 - 3

WATER USE MATH • page 61

1. 3 gallons, 30 gallons 210 gallons
2. 15 gallons, 105 gallons
3. 13 gallons
4. 150 gallons
5. 84 gallons, 48 gallons, 36 gallons

A WATERY PUZZLE • page 62

1. reservoir
2. environment
3. saturation
4. impurities
5. disinfection
6. irrigation
7. aquifer
8. industry
9. coagulation
10. filtration
11. precipitation

word: EVAPORATION

WATER QUICK CHECK • page 63

1. purified
2. reservoir
3. sewage
4. effluent
5. quotas
6. evaporation
7. industry
8. YES
9. NO
10. NO
11. NO
12. YES
13. YES
14. NO

AN AIR WORD SEARCH • page 64

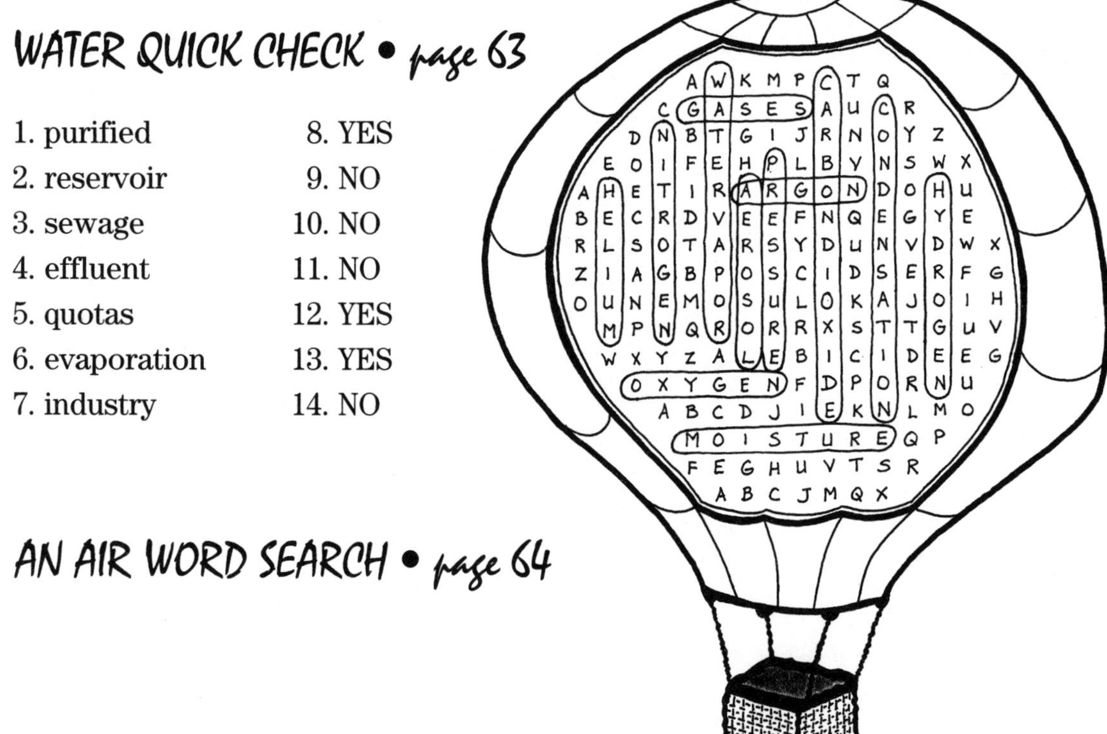

I NEED SOME AIR • page 66

1. blanket
2. planet
3. air
4. live
5. earth's
6. escaping
7. temperatures
8. earth
9. and
10. harmful

IN THE AIR • page 67

1. and
2. air
3. gas
4. oxygen
5. gases
6. time
7. water
8. vapor
9. humidity
10. aerosols

UP IN THE AIR • page 68-69

1. thermosphere (space shuttle)
2. mesosphere (50 miles; meteors)
3. stratosphere (30 miles; airplanes, ozone layer)
4. troposphere (6-10 miles; you, clouds)
5. atmosphere

WEATHER AND THE ATMOSPHERE • page 70-71

Ready:

1. meteorologist
2. mass
3. troposphere
4. vapor
5. moisture
6. temperature

Go:

1. troposphere
2. humidity
3. No
4. moderates
5. not
6. Meteorologists

ATMOSPHERIC PRESSURE • page 72-73

A. oceans
B. land
C. cool air
D. warm air
E. sun

1. molecules
2. the same
3. 15
4. air
5. inversion

OUR CHANGING CLIMATE • page 74-75

Ready:

1. tilt
2. glacier
3. atmosphere
4. altitude
5. unequal
6. orbit

Go:

1. climate
2. Yes
3. atmosphere
4. sun, atmosphere, oceans
5. they affect our ability to grow
6. people's

AN "AIRY" PUZZLE • page 82

1. molecules
2. weather
3. water vapor
4. absorb
5. ozone
6. greenhouse
7. humidity
8. air
9. aerosols
10. oxygen
11. climate
12. altitude
13. pressure

AIR QUICK CHECK • *page 83*

1. atmosphere
2. troposphere
3. barometer
4. nitrogen
5. humidity
6. aerosols
7. heat
8. YES
9. NO
10. YES
11. YES
12. YES
13. YES
14. YES

SECTION THREE: ECOLOGY

A PLANT WORD SEARCH • *page 86*

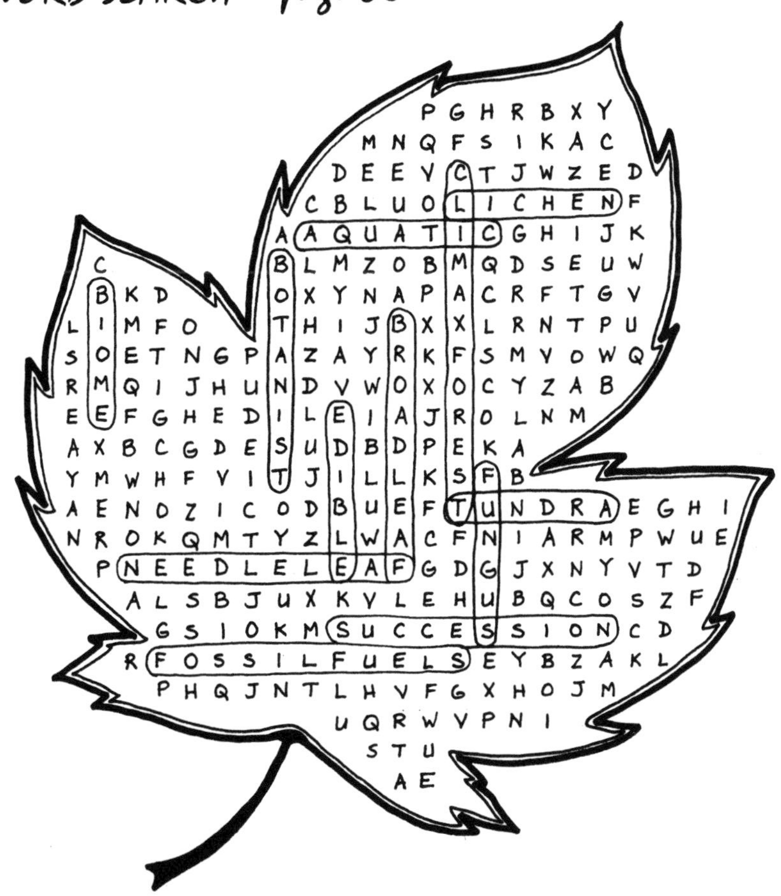

THE GREEN PROVIDERS • page 88

1. things
2. around
3. color
4. and
5. from
6. plant
7. think
8. eat
9. materials
10. plants

PLANT SURVIVAL • page 89

1. Earth
2. Plants
3. themselves
4. plants
5. they
6. prickles
7. eat
8. developed
9. smells
10. flower

PLANT SUCCESSION • page 94-95

Ready:

1. spores
2. Photosynthesis
3. fungus
4. violently
5. rhyzoids
6. seedlings

Go:

1. slowly
2. sunshine, shade
3. lichen
4. YES
5. climax
6. grasses
7. grasses and other thin-leaved plants
8. ferns

SPECIAL PARTS, SPECIAL JOBS • *page 96-97*

1. stamen
2. pistal
3. flower
4. petal
5. sepal
6. leaf
7. stem
8. root

Most chlorophyll is in the plant's leaves. Chlorophyll helps the plant make food.

BIOME RIDDLES • *page 98-99*

1. forest biome
2. tundra biome
3. desert biome
4. grasslands biome

TROPICAL TREASURE • *page 100-101*

Ready:

1. lush
2. exported
3. mahogany and teak
4. tropical
5. temporarily
6. combined

Go:

1. hot
2. 12 hours
3. answers will vary
4. slash and burn
5. millions
6. 50%
7. NO

SCRAMBLED TREES • page 102

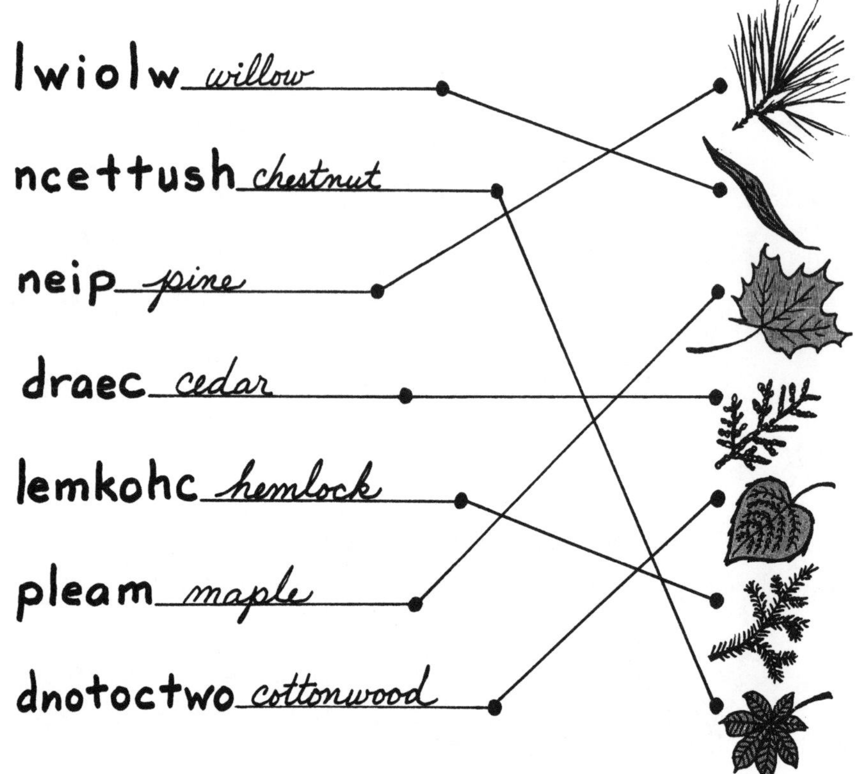

Broadleaf: willow, chestnut, maple, cottonwood
Needleleaf: pine, cedar, hemlock

TRANSPIRATION • page 103

1 - 3 - 4 - 5 - 2 - 6
*transpiration

HOW TALL? • page 104

1. 30 feet
2. 45 feet
3. 80 feet
4. 100 feet
5. 35 feet
6. 285 feet
7. 65 feet
8. 20 feet

PLANTS QUICK CHECK • *page 105*

1. chlorophyll
2. biomes
3. Transpiration
4. succession
5. Lichen
6. Photosynthesis
7. flower
8. YES
9. NO
10. NO
11. NO
12. YES
13. NO
14. YES

AN ANIMAL WORD SEARCH • *page 106*

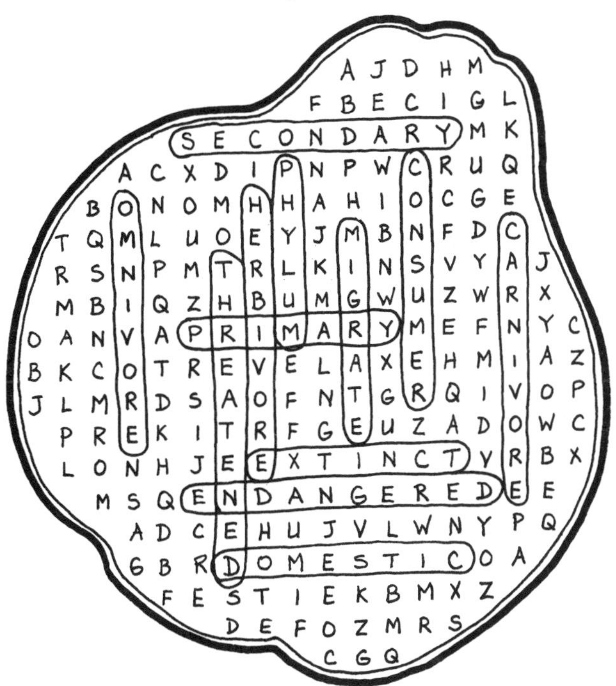

ANIMALS, ANIMALS, ANIMALS • *page 108*

1. well
2. long
3. environment
4. plants
5. eat
6. Animals
7. move
8. animals
9. breathe
10. earth

CLASSIFYING ANIMALS • page 109

1. many
2. animal
3. grouped
4. classify
5. groups
6. animals
7. belong
8. and
9. dog
10. system

BATTLE FOR SURVIVAL • page 110-111

Ready:

1. Scarce
2. exhausted
3. Adaptability
4. hibernate
5. camouflage
6. habitat

Go:

1. everywhere
2. food, water and a place to raise young
3. YES
4. hibernate
5. camouflage/change color
6. protection
7. adapt

THE CLEAN-UP CREW • page 114-115

Ready:

1. cycle
2. predator
3. scavenger
4. compost, humus
5. carcass

Go:

1. NO
2. nutrients
3. decomposers
4. cycle
5. scavengers
6. Plants

EXOTIC INVADERS • *page 122*

1. NO
2. NO
3. YES
4. YES
5. YES

AN ANIMAL PUZZLE • *page 123*

Across:

2. cow
3. marine mammal
5. killer whale
8. bear
9. primate
10. camel
11. rodent

Down:

1. carnivore
2. chimpanzee
3. marsupials
4. monkey
6. animals
7. baboon

ANIMAL LIFE SPANS • *page 124*

1. 30 years
2. 75 years
3. horse, hippopotomus
   chimpanzee, elephant, human
4. dog
5. cat, dog, squirrel, mouse
6. 35 years
7. 37 years
8. 15 years
9. 35 years

ANIMAL QUICK CHECK • *page 125*

1. adapt
2. zoologists
3. habitat
4. domestic
5. phylum
6. decomposers
7. niche
8. YES
9. YES
10. NO
11. YES
12. YES
13. NO
14. NO

A WORD SEARCH ABOUT PEOPLE • *page 126*

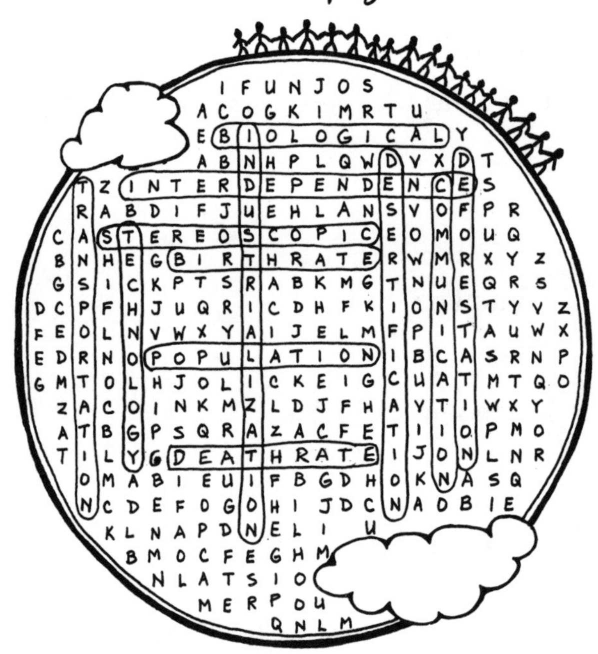

A LITTLE HISTORY • *page 128*

1. highly
2. people
3. eat
4. animals
5. food
6. planting
7. crops
8. food
9. hunting
10. work

A LITTLE CULTURE • *page 129*

1. clothing	6. is
2. wear	7. part
3. world	8. customs
4. answer	9. way
5. different	10. parents

WE ARE UNIQUE • *page 130-131*

Ready:

1. Unique	4. curious
2. Upright	5. Opposable
3. adaptable, flexible	6. complex, intricate

Go:

1. air, water, food, shelter	4. thumbs
2. larger	5. yes
3. stereoscopic	6. speech, *answers will vary

WORLD POPULATION GROWTH • *page 132-133*

1. 5.4 billion
2. less than 10 years
3. population increase
4. children helped with chores, increased chance of some children surviving; adult children would care for parents in old age
5. improvement in food production

*Answers will vary

WHERE ARE ALL THE PEOPLE? • *page 134-135*

1. NO	4. YES
2. YES	5. YES
3. NO	6–10. Answers will vary.

WHAT ARE WE DOING? • page 136-137

Ready:

1. grassland
2. habitat
3. impact
4. desertification
5. population

Go:

1. YES
2. resources
3. The soil is poor.
4. desertification
5. Answers will vary.
6. air; water

SURPRISE SLOGAN • page 142

WE ARE EARTH SMART

LIFE EXPECTANCY • page 144

1. 25 years
2. 12 years
3. 9 years
4. Africa, Asia, South America, North America, Europe, Australia

PEOPLE QUICK CHECK • page 145

1. opposable
2. agriculture
3. Culture
4. unique
5. language
6. population
7. Deforestation
8. NO
9. YES
10. NO
11. NO
12. NO
13. NO
14. YES

SECTION FOUR: CONSERVATION

ENERGY WORD SEARCH • page 148

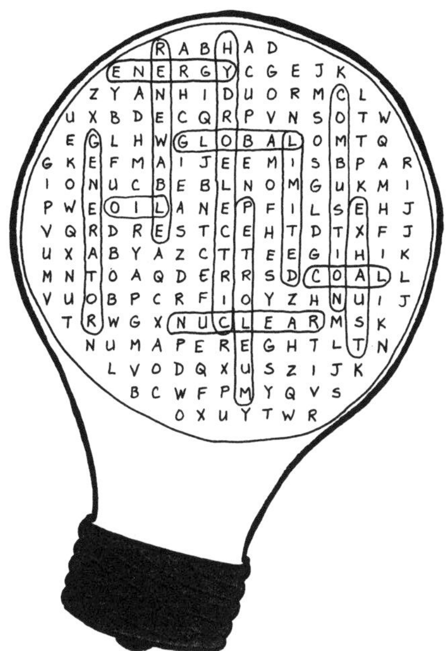

ENERGY FOR THE EARTH • page 150

1. drank
2. energy
3. need
4. first
5. sun's
6. store
7. stored
8. fuels
9. people
10. many

MORE AND MORE ENERGY • page 151

1. fuels
2. used
3. these
4. more
5. people
6. energy
7. things
8. energy
9. hands
10. amount

FOSSIL FUELS • page 152-153

Ready:

1. prehistoric
2. global
3. drought
4. failure
5. petroleum
6. sulfuric acid

Go:

1. 90%
2. NO
3. carbon dioxide
4. *any two of the following:* drought, flood, crop failure
5. sulfur dioxide
6. The sulfur dioxide mixes with the raindrops.

ALTERNATIVE ENERGY SOURCES • page 154-155

Ready:

1. hydroelectric
2. alternative
3. Fossil fuels
4. nuclear
5. Limited, renewable
6. generator

Go:

1. fossil fuels
2. alternative
3. YES
4. radioactive waste, nuclear accidents
5. *any two of the following:* tides, waves, wind
6. conservation

MAKING ELECTRICITY • page 156-157

1. turbine
2. fuel
3. boiler
4. condenser
5. generator
6. transformer

CARS, CARS, CARS • *page 160-161*

1. Automobiles
2. trains
3. choose
4. steam-powered
5. gas-powered
6. engines
7. inside
8. explosions
9. exhaust
10. affordable
11. pollution
12. fossil fuels

METER READER • *page 164*

1. 7962
2. 4303 kilowatt-hours

WHAT R-U? • *page 165*

ENERGY SMART

POWERFUL PROBLEMS • *page 166*

1. 13,053 pounds of carbon dioxide
2. 45 watts; 270 watts; 98,550 watts
3. 35 gallons; 20 gallons
4. 36,000 watts; 18,000 watts; 6,570,000 watts (or 6,570 kilowatts)

ENERGY QUICK CHECK • *page 167*

1. energy
2. fossil fuels
3. prehistoric
4. carbon dioxide
5. fission
6. Hydroelectric
7. engines
8. YES
9. NO
10. YES
11. NO
12. YES
13. YES
14. YES

A POLLUTION WORD SEARCH • page 168

WHAT IS POLLUTION? • page 170

1. natural
2. environment
3. polluted
4. few
5. could
6. change
7. more
8. pollution
9. not
10. want

WHAT A MESS! • page 171

1. causes
2. unfit
3. activities
4. large
5. pollute
6. natural
7. area
8. pollution
9. rain
10. lakes

WHAT'S IN THE AIR? • page 172-173

Ready:

1. vehicles
2. ozone
3. monitor
4. pollutants
5. aerosol
6. thermal

Go:

1. greenhouse
2. NO
3. fossil fuels
4. protects from ultraviolet rays
5. inversion
6. weather changes, food shortage

WHAT'S IN THE AIR? • page 174-175

Ready:

1. Hull
2. Petroleum
3. sewage
4. Pesticides; chemicals
5. industries
6. dramatic

Go:

1. 100
2. *any three of the following:* oil, chemicals, sewage, heat
3. YES
4. thermal
5. Oil
6. Sewage treatment; laws to limit dumping of waste into waterways

HOUSEHOLD HAZARDS • page 178-179

1. *any five of the following:* bleach, paint, motor oil, batteries, window cleaner (or others)
2. poison, corrosive, flammable, warning, caution (or others)
3. *any three of the following:* make people sick, cause burns, ignite fires, poisonous, fumes, explosions (or others)
4. They don't know the right way to dispose of the toxics. They think a small amount won't matter.

NOISE, NOISE, NOISE! • page 184

1. whisper
2. talking
3. vacuum cleaner
4. rock band
5. jet plane
6. rock band, jet plane
7. telephone, vacuum cleaner
8. Answers will vary.

BEACH PICKUP • page 185

Circled items: lunch box and bones; motor oil; plastic soda can holder; fish hook and line; bottle; can; soda cup and straw; spoon

POLLUTION PROBLEMS • page 186

1. 285 lbs. of CO_2
2. 1,150,000 animals
3. 3,900,000 trees
4. 31,500 pesticides
5. 100 gallons of water; 5200 gallons of water

POLLUTION QUICK CHECK • page 187

1. Pollution
2. acid rain
3. ozone
4. greenhouse
5. wastes
6. Pesticides
7. hazardous
8. YES
9. NO
10. YES
11. NO
12. NO
13. YES
14. NO

WANTED: EARTH SMART PEOPLE • *page 188*

```
A I C M P E O F R S C B O P S U T
J B L D C O N S E R V A T I O N W
H K P N O Q G Y A B D N Q R X V Z
S T O R M D R A I N S N E Y C A G
A V L T P X E Z J L I E B D F R W
N U L W O G S H K H J D Q U R V S
I E U F S I P P M Z S A X T U E C
T K T L T R O N O D O Y J D N B H
A M I N L A N D F I L L F I O G K
R J O B K D S H F S I J M C F H A
Y A N I C G I E I P D L E N F B D
Q B R O K P B H T O W J X E Z B C
A D U R A B L E U S A W F Y G D A
L I F C S M E V I A S Z I S K U M
A H D C K P N F Q L T H T J B L W
G E B J D E O N G R E A Y D V X C
```

WHY DO WE POLLUTE? • *page 190*

1. greatly
2. reasons
3. environment
4. pesticides
5. number
6. waste
7. pollutants
8. sulfur
9. throwing
10. reused

RACHEL CARSON • *page 191*

1. years
2. knew
3. looked
4. sea
5. books
6. called
7. think
8. near
9. dangers
10. didn't

DOWN IN THE DUMPS • page 192-193

Ready:

1. groundwater
2. solid
3. reserve
4. Leach
5. foul
6. Wastes

Go:

1. Yes
2. contaminate
3. sanitary landfills
4. air
5. valuable materials are sorted out of the garbage
6. landfills

THE THREE R'S • page 194-195

Ready:

1. incinerator
2. over-package
3. durable
4. charity
5. Aluminum
6. Researchers

Go:

1. incinerators; landfills
2. 80%
3. reduce, reuse, recycle
4. unnecessary layers of packaging materials
5. recycled
6. Answers will vary.

WHAT'S COMPOST? • page 204

1. NO
2. YES
3. NO
4. NO
5. YES
6. YES

A CONSERVATION PUZZLE • *page* 205

1. contaminate
2. durable
3. waste
4. healthier
5. runoff
6. disposal
7. technology
8. sanitary
9. Recycle
10. conservation

Puzzle solution: EARTH SMART

A LITTLE LOGIC • *page* 206

GLASS — Kate
NEWSPAPER — Barbara
ALUMINUM — Maria
TIN CAN — Jamal
MIXED PAPER — Mike

CONSERVATION QUICK CHECK • *page* 207

1. recycle
2. resources
3. technology
4. Runoff
5. Pesticides
6. landfills
7. responsibility
8. YES
9. YES
10. NO
11. NO
12. YES
13. NO
14. NO